People and Places
in
Upper Wharfedale

*A collection of articles written by members
of the Upper Wharfedale Field Society's
Local History Group
1990 – 2005.*

Brontë Bedford-Payne

Compiled by Brontë Bedford-Payne.

Edited by Helen Wheatley.

David Francis

Book cover and line drawings by David Francis.

Waymarkers drawn by Phyllida Oates.

Bronte Bedford-Payne

First Published in Great Britain in 2007 by

Summers Barn Publishing

The moral right of the author(s) has been asserted.

Printed in the U.K. by Lamberts P&D, Settle.

Typesetting, layout and artwork by

Phil Hudson. Hudson History, Procter House, Settle.

British Library Cataloguing in Publication Data.

A catalogue record of this book is available from the British Library.

ISBN: 978-0-9554166-0-6

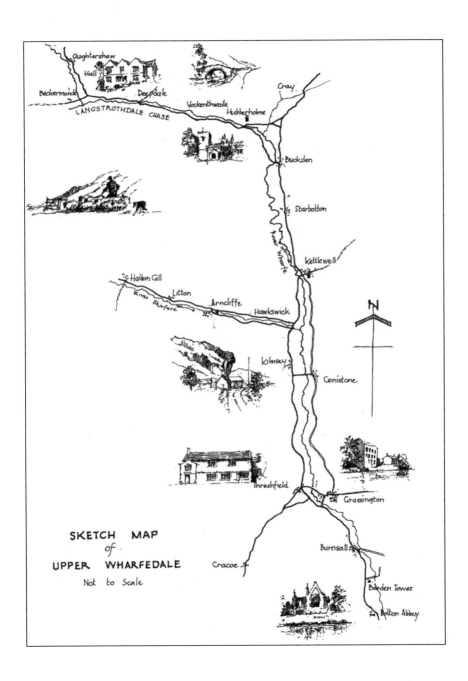

Oughtershaw
Hall
Beckermonds
Deepdale
LANGSTROTHDALE CHASE
Yockenthwaite
Hubberholme
Cray
Buckden
Starbotton
River Wharfe
Kettlewell
Halton Gill
Litton
River Skirfare
Arncliffe
Hawkswick
Kilnsey
Conistone
N
Threshfield
Grassington
Burnsall
Cracoe
Barden Tower
Bolton Abbey

SKETCH MAP
of
UPPER WHARFEDALE
Not to Scale

The Benedicite of The Dales

Bless the Lord all created things, praise him and rejoice
forever.
Bless the Lord all hills and mountains,
Bless the Lord all crags and scars of millstone grit and
Yoredale screes.

Bless the Lord all sparkling waters, becks, streams and
ghylls;
Bless the Lord all rushing mighty torrents that today are,
and tomorrow are but trickling peacefulness;
Bless the Lord all falls and forces gathering strength and
power from hills above.

Bless the Lord all birds of the air winging your way across
hills and dales;
Bless the Lord all curlews of graceful flight and rippling song
announcing the arrival of spring;
Bless the Lord all moorland grouse running and darting
through purple heather;
Bless the Lord all handsome dippers bobbing white-throated
in fast-running streams;

Bless the Lord all aptly named wagtails running and
dancing - pied, grey and yellow;
Bless the Lord all birds of prey soaring and diving midst
thermals and space.

Bless the Lord all plants of the earth growing in harmony to
enhance the land;
Bless the Lord all flowers of the north, bird's-eye primrose so
clear and bright, mountain pansy and bellflowers so tall;
Bless the Lord all trees of the earth - tall, proud or stunted,
leaning with the wind;
Bless the Lord all lichens and mosses – signs of pure air to
refresh the tired soil.

Bless the Lord all sheep that graze peacefully across hills
and meadows with lambs so close at heel;
Bless the Lord all sheep dogs as you willingly gather and
herd at the call of the shepherd.
Bless the Lord all you dales in variety and splendour.
Praise Him and rejoice forever!

Dorothy Peake (1935 - 1998)
Published by kind permission of
Mike Peake

Acknowledgements

I am indebted to my friends in the Upper Wharfedale Field Society who have supported me throughout the compilation of this book, and in particular to Heather Beaumont, through whom in 1989 the Local History Group was formed. It was through Heather's encouragement that the articles by Helen Le Fèvre, Martha Kneale and Bill Rhodes came to be written and presented to the Group. I thank the many friends in the Society who have granted permission to quote from their texts and reproduce photographs, each of which are individually acknowledged throughout the volume.

I am grateful to those who have allowed their work to be edited and included in the collection, and to Colin and Sheila Ginger who transcribed the text of Jacqueline Keighley's article from her lecture notes, and also the text of Martha Kneale's article from a tape recording of an informal talk she gave to the Local History Group.

I thank Jean Booth, who worked jointly with another Society member, June Tingey, to compile A Preliminary Report on the Enclosure Act for Grassington dated 1792 and its Effect on the Medieval Landscape (UWFS Archives) which was used, along with other unpublished material, as a source of reference. I thank also Christine Chisholm who provided the original report on the history of the Congregational Church. Special thanks to Wendy Fallon and Rosemary Baker who generously subedited the script, to Ruth Camm for her constructive criticism and help with some of the text, and to Phyllida Oates whose encouragement and share in the publication of this book has been invaluable.

I am indebted to Helen Wheatley, who has tirelessly and generously edited the work.

Brontë Bedford-Payne

Contents

Illustrations

Introduction

Writing in 1979, our founder member, Arthur Raistrick, said

'No society could have a finer location than Craven and the Yorkshire Dales for every kind of interest it may wish to pursue, and I have every confidence that the Society will continue to make its humble but important contribution to the expansion of our knowledge of these areas.'

Subjects contained within this book cover the area with which the Field Society is associated, from Bolton Bridge to the sources of the Wharfe and the river Skirfare. This collection of articles, written by a few members of the Upper Wharfedale Field Society, is offered as a very small cross section and yet an infinitely valuable insight into some of the private passions which absorb their interests and their time.

A great deal of social history has been included alongside information about, for instance, such essentials as the first supplies of electricity and water to the village of Grassington and the many personalities who were associated with these industrial processes. Other articles concern the water powered mills, now long gone and but a faint memory in the imagination of only a few. These are memories of grinding corn, spinning cotton, weaving worsted, or making butter, where water courses were harnessed, and wheels rotated noisily on the gable ends of sturdy buildings. Other writers have been interested in the coming of religious non-conformity in the Dale, when the building of chapels for Congregational Independents, and later for Primitive and Wesleyan Methodists, were significant events in the spiritual lives of ordinary folk. There is also a history of Quaker Meetings for Worship and the visits of George Fox to Scarhouse, above Hubberholme. Education in the Dale aroused the interest of one enthusiast, who has written about the scholars of Threshfield School who went to St John's College, Cambridge. Then we have a biography of a long-lived daleswoman, Helen Ward, daughter of a gamekeeper at Malham Tarn. She was a much loved member of the Society at the time when Arthur Raistrick was inspiring so much local interest. Family diaries, too, found a place when we wrote the history of the Woodd family in the remote hamlet of Oughtershaw. You might have peered through the bars of the iron gates by the side of their mysterious house, and wondered who lived there in its heyday.

Have you ever thought about what members of a local history group do when they are not out and about with their cameras and notebooks, prowling about old buildings, looking at such things as masons' marks under bridges or on medieval pillars in churches and abbeys? Have you ever joined them in the local reference library or the County Record Office, or on a town or village walkabout? We hope that by reading our book you, the readers, might discover for yourselves some of the delights and disappointments which come with the study of local history, and that you might find inspiration in exploring Upper Wharfedale with the added interest our researches should provide.

Brontë Bedford-Payne

> *'We shall not cease from exploration*
> *And the end of all our exploring*
> *Will be to arrive from where we started*
> *And know the place for the first time.*
> *Through the unknown, remembered gate*
> *When the last of earth left to discover*
> *Is that which was the beginning;*
> *At the source of the longest river*
> *The voice of the hidden waterfall*
> *And the children in the apple tree*
> *Not known because not looked for*
> *But heard, half heard, in the stillness'*

T.S.Eliot
From 'The Four Quartets: Little Gidding'
Faber and Faber Ltd

Burnsall/Thorpe Junction

People and Social History

Queen Victoria's Jubilee Memorial, Oughtershaw.

1. The Woodd Family Of Oughtershaw

The development of a small Victorian estate

Brontë Bedford-Payne

NON NOBIS

In a remote outreach of Wharfedale, where the river rises in an area of peat bogs and open moorland, the hamlet of Oughtershaw became home to Basil George Woodd and his family in 1847. The original seat of the Woodd family in the mid 14th century had been Holly Hall, between Barnsley and Penistone in the County of York. The Woodds were prominent in Yorkshire and in London in the legal profession, as ministers of religion, and in missionary work overseas, while Basil George Woodd (Fig. 1) was a successful wine importer in London, who had already earned the title 'Father of the Wine Trade'. He may have been familiar with Upper Wharfedale through marriage in 1814 to Mary Mitton, whose family lived in Harrogate and owned mineral rights in Starbotton and Kettlewell.

Oughtershaw stands on the site of one of seven forest lodges in Langstrothdale Chase, which was initially held by the Percy family of Northumberland, and then by the Cliffords, Earls of Cumberland. In the late 15th century there were six tenements in the hamlet:

'Oughtershaw is a hamlet in the chapelry of St. Michael's Hubberholme, in the parish of Arncliffe. It formed in ancient days a part of Langstrothdale Chase ... and stands just where the ancient copse wood ceases, and open moor commences, although numerous stems of trees, mostly birch, are met with in the peat bogs higher up the dale.' [1]

The peat bogs have revealed many interesting finds over the years. These

Fig. 1. Basil Woodd

include a curious implement of oak inscribed 'TM 1663' and numerous 14th to 17th century Scottish and English coins, suggesting that this area was once crossed by an established trade route between Yorkshire, Carlisle and Scotland.

'Until 1849 Oughtershaw was a stinted pasture, with limited rights of pasturage to the owners of old enclosures.' [2]

The Parliamentary Act of Enclosure for dividing and enclosing these stinted pastures, then known as Cow Close and Moss or West Pasture, is dated 1845, and was followed by the Award on 5th July 1849. It was during this critical time of change in the landscape that Basil Woodd acquired the farmhouse, some parcels of land, and an existing school, from Messrs. Lodge, Foster, Atkinson and Drake.[3] The transformation of the countryside which took place at that time was not an unusual occurrence during the early Victorian period. In Craven, as elsewhere in Britain, wealthy landowners such as the Dukes of Devonshire at Bolton Abbey were developing their estates by rebuilding their farmsteads and establishing sporting rights over their woods and moorlands. At the same time, following the industrial revolution, the rising prosperity of manufacturers and merchants led them to seek a style of life suited to their newly acquired affluence. They sought small estates on which they, too, could rear and shoot game birds, and build lodges where their families might enjoy the privileges of leisure and entertain their friends in spectacular surroundings of great beauty. For instance, in the neighbourhood of Oughtershaw, Colonel Garnett Orme, of Low Greenfield, and Sir John Charles Ramsden of Buckden, followed in 1879 by Colonel Crompton Stansfield, [4] each developed the land and buildings on the estates they had acquired during this period.

'At various times during the fifty years following their first purchase, the Woodds acquired the whole Oughtershaw estate of 4000 acres.' [5]

Later entries in a diary kept by the Woodds referred to further acquisitions, suggesting that ownership was not completed until nearly a century after their first venture in 1847. In 1850 Basil began substantial work on rebuilding the old farmhouse to convert it into a shooting lodge,

'in the prevailing style of the old manor houses of the country, the late Tudor style ...the stone mullioned windows giving a more than ordinary character to the humblest buildings' [6]

The plans were drawn up by Basil's son Charles, with Ewan Christian of London as architect.

'there were remains of some ancient tenement on the site, although nothing of importance..the old farmhouses mostly date from about 1640-1680. The deeds contain some of the original grants signed by Francis Lord Clifford in the reign of Charles II.' [fn1]

Fn1. Whitaker appears to be in error here, since Francis Lord Clifford died in 1641 during the reign of Charles I.

The remote situation of Oughtershaw, over 1000 ft above sea level at the head of Wharfedale, might not have aroused Basil's interest had it not been for the impending arrival of a branch railway from the main line at Northallerton to Leyburn in Wensleydale. The railway station opened in 1856, and by 1876 the line had been extended to Hawes.[7] It may be supposed that many of the materials for the building renovations were hauled up the steep rough track which led, in some places precipitously, from Hawes via Gayle, through Sleddale, over the watershed at Fleet Moss and from there down to the site of the Hall. The family and their friends and employees travelled this way in horse-drawn carriages until long after the First World War, when a motor car was first mentioned in a diary kept by members of the family whilst staying in Oughtershaw.

Fig. 2. Oughtershaw Hall

It is interesting to consider how the growing rail network in the area would have affected the development of other nearby estates: it is said locally, for instance, that the Garnett Orme family, when travelling from their home at Tarn Hows, Stirton, a hamlet on the outskirts of Skipton, to their sporting estate at Low Greenfield, 'always came along the old green road.'[8] This former pack-horse track, linking the Wharfe and Ribble valleys, followed an ancient routeway which, in the 19th century, came to provide a direct link between the Greenfield estate and the Midland Railway, completed in 1876 between Skipton and Carlisle, with a station at Horton-in-Ribblesdale.

The difficulty of maintaining this old road became apparent when it fell into disrepair. From July 1868 onwards, the minutes for the Settle Highways Board record that both Charles Woodd and Colonel Garnett Orme regularly complained to the Surveyor, and in 1878 summoned the Waywarden over the state of the road. However, despite repeated efforts on behalf of the landowners, it is evident that this contentious matter continued to be a source of irritation for decades, and it had not been favourably resolved by the last recorded entry, 16th December 1930:

'... *from Oughtershaw in Langstrothdale to Horton by way of Beckermonds and Greenfield, the road, being private property, and having been made under the powers of an act of parliament, the Board had no powers over it. It should, therefore, be repaired by Ratione Tenurae* [Fn1] *and not the Township.'* [9]

Charles Henry Lardner Woodd, (Fig. 3) who became Justice of the Peace for the West Riding of Yorkshire, was the third son of Basil and Mary Woodd. He was born in London in 1821, and inherited the Oughtershaw estate from his father in 1852. When the building of his house was complete, it became known as Oughtershaw Hall. It was:

' ... *built on a site overlooking the River Wharfe where it falls over its rocky bed, in a highly romantic ghyll, or valley, clothed with flourishing plantations.'* [10] (see Fig. 2)

A generation later, Charles' elder daughter Winifred apparently spent many hours sitting on a tree stump contemplating this ghyll, and so, for the family, it came to be named after her – Winifred's Ghyll. Charles' affinity with the spirit of the place is reflected in the wording he had carved across the front of the house:

GOD'S PROVIDENCE IS MINE
INHERITANCE. CHLW.

WHEREFORE LET THERE BE SUNG NON
NOBIS AND TE DEUM.

COME LOVE AND HEALTH TO ALL.

WELCOME AS THE FLOWERS IN SPRING.

When Charles occupied the Hall, the enclosing, reclaiming, draining and liming of some 700 acres of the old allotments was begun, and two farms,

Fig. 3. Charles Woodd

Fn1. Ratione Tenurae: applies when a public carriage way is maintainable by adjoining landowners instead of by the Local Authority.

5

'each of over 1000 acres, were established on the improved land, and soon yielded good meadow hay where of old only coarse herbage and rough sheep-pasture existed'. [11]

The work was carried out under the direction of an engineer by the name of Bowes, from the West of England Drainage Company. The implementation of such an extensive scheme in the marshy valley surrounding the many springs from which the Wharfe and the Ribble arise must have seemed a remarkable enterprise to local people. There were three possible factors which might have influenced Basil and Charles Woodd to embark on their policy of land drainage and reclamation. Firstly, in 1840 an Act of Parliament allowed landowners to raise money for drainage by making a heritable debt on the estate. This was followed by the Public Money Drainage Act of 1846, which made government money available at a low rate of interest. [12] Whether or not Basil Woodd availed himself of such a loan is not recorded, but it is likely that he would have been aware of its existence at the time when he bought the land in 1847. Secondly, he might well have been aware of the improvements made during the previous century by Thomas Elliott of Fremington, in the neighbouring tributary valley of Greenfield, whereby, through enclosure, drainage, and cultivation,

'the black moorland soil ...turns out a very good, profitable pasture ... two acres of it will carry a cow thro' summers well'. (Appendix A.)

Thirdly, it is possible that their friendship with John Ruskin prompted the Woodds to fulfil some of the ideals which, some twenty years later, led Ruskin to form the Guild of St George:

'In 1871 John Ruskin purchased Brantwood in Cumbria at a time which coincided with his setting up of the 'Guild of St George' through which he encouraged people to assist in the purchase of neglected or barren land which could be reclaimed for cultivation.

Ruskin's concern for the social and economic poverty in which many people lived formed part of the more ambitious scheme to carry out a series of practical projects using the natural resources of his new estate at Brantwood. He wished to discover ways in which such marginal land could best be used both to appease hunger and to cultivate the minds and thoughts of the labourers'. [13]

Fig. 4. The Memorial Chapel at Oughtershaw

Tragedy had struck in 1856 with the death of Charles' first wife, Lydia Wilson Sole, who died from tuberculosis at the age of thirty-two, while attending a special clinic in Pau. She left two daughters, Winifred Maria aged three, and Mary Bianca, aged two. A year later a Memorial Chapel, (Fig. 4) probably designed by John Ruskin, was founded and built by Charles who, together with Lydia's parents, John and Ada Sole, placed an inscription above the entrance door. (Fig. 5)

Fig. 5. Lydia's Memorial

Fig. 6. The Entrance to the Chapel

'Good use was made of various Yorkshire stones, with the main body being built from well-dressed sandstone bricks. Courses of red fine-grained sandstone were laid at intervals along the main wall, adding a little colour, although these layers weather more quickly than the gritstone. Limestone was used for the more ornate structures that grace windows and entrance, and the finegrained stone of the door columns gives the appearance of possibly two different limestones. Most elaborate of all is the polished fossiliferous limestone used for the window pillars, porch paving and wall plaques.

Most of this was probably quarried at Dent, and is known as Dent Marble. The unique patterns are the fossils of crinoids or sea lilies. One of the plaques shows fossils of solitary corals, and resembles the Frosterly Marble, which was quarried in Weardale. Neither is true marble, but both rocks take a good polish and were much in demand for decorative purposes.' [14] *(Fig. 6).*

In 1864 Charles married his second wife, Jane Harris of Leicester, by whom he had two sons, Trevor Basil and Charles Hampden Basil, and two daughters, Gertrude and Ethel. A strong commitment to Christian causes was evident in the whole family, each member featuring in the life and events at Oughtershaw. Missionary meetings, addressed by Charles, were held annually in the Memorial Chapel, and sales of work were held in the Hall grounds to raise funds for the Church Missionary Society, while Jane not only provided splendid teas, but also gifts of books for the children. By 1872 two new farmhouses, Swarthghyll and Netherghyll, had been built at Oughtershaw (Fig 7). Each had an elegant staircase, a spacious hall, kitchens and two reception rooms.

Substantial stone barns and outbuildings around the farmyards provided ample shelter and accommodation for crops and animals, indicating a high degree of confidence in the productivity of these newly established farms. Christopher (Kitty) Wallace Foster, a direct descendant of the Foster and Lodge families of Oughtershaw and Beckermonds, took over Netherghyll in April of that year. Miss Florence Foster Brook recounts the tale of how, from Netherghyll, Kitty's

Fig. 7. Swarthghyll

eighteen year-old granddaughter, Mary Ann Chapman, eloped with the village schoolmaster, Mr. Jelphs, 'this, of course, caused a great stir at the time'. [15] Later, one of Kitty's daughters, Ann, farmed at Swarthghyll with her husband William Lambert.

In 1874 Charles and Jane completed further additions to the Hall. To celebrate this, all the tenants were invited to a special dinner in the warm, hospitable new dining room.

In the following years there was a progressive programme of tree planting in small copses and larger plantations. Many trees grew to full maturity despite the adverse weather conditions prevailing in such an exposed situation. They endured exceptionally heavy rains, gales and prolonged snowstorms, and on 14th January 1933, an earthquake. Inevitably, there were casualties among the growing trees, some of which the family recorded in their diary: when a whirlwind swept from Askrigg over Cray S.W. to Ingleton causing a line of devastation some fifty yards wide across the valley, rooting up many large forest trees '… some fifty to sixty large forest trees in Todd's Wood near Hubberholme church … many trees rent and splintered…'

'1899 March 24th. Whilst burning ling in the far plantation at Swarthghyll the fire 'got away' and was only finally extinguished by a snow shower. The whole of the Moss was ruined, no heather survived and plantations of thirty years' growth were utterly destroyed.' [16]

Charles suffered another family tragedy in 1882, the death in London of his 28 year old daughter Mary Bianca, only six weeks after her marriage. However, his care of the community never seemed to be hindered by personal grief, and his deep faith prevailed. He continued to contribute unfailingly to the many needs of the parish, including church restoration and upkeep in Hubberholme, Kettlewell and Arncliffe. His brothers, when visiting, delivered sermons at one or other of these churches, while the female members of the family concerned themselves with floral church decorations for festivals. Harvest provided an abundance of flowers, fruit and corn, which would later be sent down to the Orphanage of Mercy at Kilburn. Each Christmas the children of Oughtershaw were treated to a party at the school and sometimes visitors to the Hall invited the local children to tea. The parish magazine for November 1887 records an invitation to tea at the pleasure of Colonel and Mrs. Mersey-Thompson, when the Colonel *'delivered an instructive lecture upon the Ashanti War in West Africa in 1873 in which he was personally engaged under Sir Garnet Wolseley.* [17]

The same issue of the magazine records how Queen Victoria's Jubilee of 1887 was marked:

'St Michael's Hubberholme - on Wednesday August 3rd - the echoes of the Queen's great Jubilee at length reached the distant village of Oughtershaw, which though last, proved not least in celebrating it. A huge block, quarried from the hillside above, was

forced to play the part of a rolling stone till it was set up on end and mounted in a socket sunk in a small weather-worn scar, just where the road turns up from Oughtershaw to Hawes ... bearing on its front, beneath a Maltese Cross within an incised circle, the famous letters 'V.R.' and the date of the Jubilee. (Fig. 8). Crowned with flowers, (it) was unveiled by one of the young ladies of the Woodd family.

'God Save the Queen' was sung by schoolchildren and others who had made a procession thither. After a loyal and patriotic address from Mr. Woodd, the whole party went to the Hall, where more than a hundred persons were liberally feasted ... As evening approached, a festoon of Chinese lanterns was suspended across the gravelled court ...and amid this glittering little fairyland the children amused each other on a swing. As darkness grew on, a charming display of very beautiful fireworks was given by Mr. Woodd and his sons ... even the moon by a gracious coincidence favoured the last scene of the festivities with an accommodating eclipse.' [18]

In the summer of 1892, Charles and Jane, with his daughters Gertrude and Ethel, visited their old friend, John Ruskin, in his home at Brantwood by Lake Coniston. Their friendship had dated from early days, when Ruskin's father and Basil Woodd had followed a similar profession in the wine trade.

By 1893 Charles' health was beginning to fail and he spent more time in London. On 15th December, aged almost 72, he died at his home in Hampstead; a tribute was published by the Craven Herald and reprinted in the parish magazine. The Christmas and New Year's festivities normally held in Oughtershaw School were cancelled, and the children did not go carol singing. However, some of the former pupils maintained the parish's established custom on Christmas Day; starting from Beckermonds, and calling at each of the farms and singing carols with concertina accompaniment, they went down Langstrothdale as far as Hubberholme Church. The following evening, setting out from Oughtershaw, they visited Netherghyll, Swarthghyll and Cam, before crossing the moor to High Greenfield, and thence to Low Greenfield on their way home. The proceeds provided for a

Fig. 8. Jubilee Commemorative Stone

10

party and a ball held at Cowside Farm in Langstrothdale for all the community.

Charles' widow Jane now remained in London but the family returned to Oughtershaw Hall for holidays and shooting parties. Trevor, their eldest son, inherited the estate, and in 1900, the writer Harry Speight recounted:

'he fully upholds all the good traditions of his parents in taking the liveliest interest in every measure calculated to improve and beautify the ancestral domain. In former years, he and his brother, Charles Hampden B. Woodd, took especial delight and devoted considerable time in studying and investigating every aspect of the grand upland country where they lived. Its geology, meteorology, botany, and natural history generally were followed and noted with the keenest interest, and some of their contributions to the 'Naturalist', particularly of the flowering plants of the district, are genuine aids to science. Some 300 species of plants have been recorded by them as flourishing within a few miles radius of Oughtershaw, including some very uncommon species as well as records of plants found at altitudes elsewhere unknown in Yorkshire. No doubt draining and planting have contributed to raise the altitudinal range of some of the species. The common sycamore, it may be noted, has been found, together with purple fox-glove, self-sown in a pot-hole near Oughtershaw Tarn, at an elevation 1,800 feet above the sea. [19]

In July 1896 the younger Charles went to Tokyo as a missionary, returning four years later to be ordained. He then resumed his work in Japan for another fifteen years. Trevor became vicar of St John's, Fitzroy Square, London, in 1911.

Entries in the Diary for the years spanning the Great War are sparse; we read nothing of the family's doings in Oughtershaw. It is possible that they closed the Hall. The death of one of their young keepers, John Turnbull Jnr., whilst fighting for his country in France, was mentioned, and his name appears on the war memorial in Hubberholme church. Also mentioned is the award of the Military Medal to George Turnbull, of Oughtershaw. During this time, in 1915, Charles returned from Japan to settle in Dorsetshire.

A local tragedy occurred in 1918 when their neighbour *'Captain Garnett Orme was killed at a shoot on Oughtershaw Moor'* [20] but, as with other entries, this one is tantalizingly brief and unaccompanied by any further comment.

On a happier note, an entry for 2nd June 1924 joyfully announced that *'Ethel G Woodd arrived as far as the middle of Beckermonds Hill in a motor car'.* [21] In 1931, Ethel again referred to changes; it seems that horse power was no longer the ultimate resource *'coming over from Hawes by car now … not the strenuous climb running beside a horse drawn trap'.* [22]

On 29th June 1927 Trevor Basil Woodd (Master of Salters' Company) *'saw total eclipse of the sun with my nephew Frederick Basil.'* [23]

A succession of agents and caretakers managed the Hall and the estate for the family. It was difficult to appoint good, dependable staff during the First World War and in the years of economic depression which followed. However, from 1927 until 1933 entries show that they were faithfully served by Mr and Mrs White *'who did much for Oughtershaw water supply, saw mill etc. … six years faithful service'.* [24]

Tree planting continued and work progressed on the Hall's private water supply, which is still in use. Community functions continued to be held at the Hall, raising funds for the upkeep of the church and school, for The Society for the Propagation of the Gospel and The Church Missionary Society. Trevor's sister Gertrude was for many years the secretary and treasurer for these good causes.

World War II brought many changes for the Woodd family. Upkeep of the hall became difficult, and slow deterioration in its fabric was evident. At the end of the war it was still hard to maintain adequate staff, and Trevor spent more time away from Oughtershaw. The final entry in the diary reads: *'1946, 10th August. The Rev. Trevor Basil Woodd, M.A., LL.B, of Oughtershaw, Vicar of St. John's, Fitzroy Square, London, 1911-1940, died at Eastbourne on March 20th 1946, aged 79 years.'* [25] The estate was then dispersed and Oughtershaw Hall was put up for sale. Eventually, the sadly neglected but still handsome old house became home to a new family, who, throughout another long period of ownership, have established their own traditions.

The remarkable 100 year era of the Woodd family is honoured in Hubberholme church by a memorial plaque to Charles Henry Lardner Woodd 1821-1893 (Fig. 9) and by stained glass windows in memory of his first wife Lydia, and his mother, Mary, wife of Basil Woodd, who died in 1864. In 1965 the stone High Altar was given by a descendant, Rev. B. Woodd. The legacy of this family's devotion to Oughtershaw is the Hall and the chapel, which became the village school room, and also the buildings and reclaimed acreages of farmland at Swarthghyll and Netherghyll. Meanwhile some scattered copses of tall, strong native trees have grown to maturity, and continue to nourish the soil with their annual fall of leaves – a perpetual reminder of the family whose love for this place endured for a century.

IN LOVING MEMORY OF
CHARLES HENRY LARDNER WOODD
OF OUGHTERSHAW HALL AND ROSLYN HOUSE HAMPSTEAD J.P.
BORN 18. DEC. 1821, DIED 15. DEC. 1893.
"THE MEMORY OF THE JUST IS BLESSED."

Fig. 9. Charles Woodd's Memorial Stone in Hubberholme Church

References

1 Whitaker, Rev TD, (1973) The History and Antiquities of the Deanery of Craven in the County of York, Third edition, Vol. II, reprinted by J.J. Morton, Didsbury, Manchester and the Craven Herald, Skipton: pp 574-5.

2 ibid.

3 ibid.

4 Cole, Don (2003) A Farm in Upper Wharfedale, Wharfedale Family History Group.

5 Whitaker 1973.

6 ibid.

7 Raistrick, Arthur, (1968), The Pennine Dales, London: Eyre and Spottiswoode, p.132.

8 Verbal communication to Brontë Bedford Payne.

9 Minutes of the Settle Highways Board (1968-1930) NYCRO 3861.

10 Whitaker 1973.

11 ibid.

12 Wade Martins, Susanna (2004), Farmers, Landlords and Landscapes, Macclesfield: Windgather Press Ltd.

13 Display board, Brantwood (2002).

14 Wilding, Royanne (2003), UWFS Geology Group.

15 Brook, Florence Foster, (1962), Reprint Beckermonds, Holborn, London. EC1: William Kempner Ltd.

16 The Oughtershaw Hall Diary 1847-1946.

17 The Upper Wharfedale Parish Magazine, (November 1887).

18 ibid.

19 Speight, Harry (1900) Upper Wharfedale, London: Elliot Stock, pp 494, 497-8.

20 Diary

21 ibid.

22 ibid.

23 ibid.

24 ibid.

25 ibid.

Source:

Long, W Harwood (1969) A Survey of the Agriculture of Yorkshire, London: Royal Agricultural Society of England.

Appendix A p138 Young, Arthur. (1770) A Farmer's Tour Through the North of England, Vol. 2, London: W. Strahan.

Acknowledgements:

Dr Wilma Keppie, of Kettlewell. (UWFS), who inspired this article, supplied her copy of The Oughtershaw Hall Diary 1847-1946 and gave us her photographs of Oughtershaw Hall.

Phyllida Oates, for research with the present owner at Oughtershaw Hall, and with Mrs Jocelyn Patterson, née Woodd (London). For her contributions to the script, and for obtaining the photographs from Thomas Ryder's Rambles in Upper Wharfedale 1867-1950 by kind permission of the author's grandson, Dr. Michael Ryder.

Mrs. Jocelyn Patterson née Woodd, who granted permission to publish extracts from The Oughtershaw Hall Diary, supplied copies of family photographs, and shared her personal memories of the Woodd family.

The present owner of Oughtershaw Hall, for her kindness in making us welcome and for permission to take and publish photographs of the Hall.

Burnsall/Thorpe Junction

2. Helen Ward,
A True Daleswoman: Portrait of a Friend

Brontë Bedford-Payne

Helen Ward (1906-1988) (Fig. 10) was a gamekeeper's daughter whose Edwardian childhood on the remote upland estate around Malham Tarn instilled in her a stoic sense of family loyalties, duty and hard work. She was the third daughter and sixth child in a family of twelve children born to Alfred and Jane Ward (née Earnshaw)

Her grandfather and father successively were gamekeepers for the millionaire Walter Morrison and their home was Sandhill Cottage, one of several in the hamlet of Waterhouses. These cottages, and two or three farmhouses on Malham Moor, had been designed and built for Walter Morrison at the end of the nineteenth century, especially for his tenants and estate workers.

Fig. 10. Helen Ward as a young woman

By all accounts her father Alf Ward was a stern and intimidating figure, who controlled all things pertaining to game on the moors and in the woods, as well as the fish in the tarn, guarding them with jealous determination, and woe betide any potential poacher.

His children roamed freely through the woods and by the tarn; they learned to recognize and identify plants, many of them wild flowers unique to the area, and to observe the habits and seasonal migrations of birds. It was here that Helen developed her affinity with the environment and the abundant wildlife around her home.

Fig. 11. Alf Ward fishing on Malham Tarn, 1920s

As she wrote in her poems, and once remarked to me "I loved to row out on the tarn. My dad taught me to row as soon as I could hold an oar. We was 'appy, then." (Figs. 12 and 13).

Fig. 12. The Ward Family, 1928

The following excerpt from 'Good Friday Walk', forms part of her collection of verse 'Small Wonders'. The poem recalls her childhood 4 with that deep sense of place and contentment which characterised her personality:

Fig. 13. Five of the Ward Children

"Let's go a walk this afternoon," our Bill he said to me.

To go a walk down by the tarn, we all agree as one.

Down into our planting we go in single file.

The tarn edge now we see, we run a bit, and jump a bit and climb upon a tree.

The wind has blown it down; its roots are not quite free

We climbed a mound of roughish ground, and there were lots of nettles.

Jimmy said "Oh, come and see t'robins nest in this old kettle".

A mallard duck, she caught my eye

She was sat quite near the path.

Then up she flew, as we passed-by.

I bend to see if she had laid

Ah yes, six blue-green eggs, cosy and warm

Resting in the feathery nest she'd made.

"Let's see if there's any Bullheads under these big stones."

We found a few, and crayfish too, in the creek by the boathouse.

A ring of hawthorns grew near there, right against the boathouse;

They made a tent-like shape; we often played in there.'

Many other poems reflect nostalgia for a way of life she knew so well, in that small cottage where the ever increasing numbers of her tightly knit family shared daily chores common to many households during the first part of the twentieth century:

Fig. 14. Malham Tarn House
Showing Italianate tower in situ before it was demolished in the late 1940s

'My childish hands were taught to write, make figures, to hold a bat
and ball.

To dust and knit, to bake, to sew, mend socks and breeches

And make use of all the stitches.

Knead the Bread before the school

Carry the Milk up to the Hall

Feed the Dogs and clean their Kennels

Feed the Hens and Feed the Ducks

Collect the Eggs, peep at the Chicks

Collect some Turf, and then gather Sticks.

My friendship with Helen came towards the end of her life, for she had been a friend of my mother's family, who were tenant farmers at Low Trenhouse on Malham Moor. By the time I met her, the Malham Tarn estate had been bequeathed to the National Trust, and Malham Tarn House (Fig. 14), the former home of Walter Morrison, had been leased to the Field Studies Council.

We had many conversations whilst sipping 'smoky' tea, flecked with soot from the kettle suspended over the fire from the iron reckan-crook [Fn1] in her Hetton kitchen, or pottering in the front garden amongst her kittens and the cottage flowers. I remember how, one July day in 1978, she arranged a delicate posy of miniature rosebuds from her garden in a tiny silver vase; I can still see her small sunburnt hand curled round its stem as she placed it carefully on my daughter's wedding cake.

Our outings were always a joy for both of us, full of comments and reminiscent chat, when time seemed to stand still. I recall a day together at Waterhouses; we moved very slowly across the boardwalk by the tarn moss while Helen pointed out different species of willow, spied an orchid and caught a glimpse of a sitting Great Crested Grebe. We stood helplessly by while a coot raided a nearby unprotected nest and systematically threw every egg into the water while the parent birds, returning from feeding, circled at a short distance, calling harshly.

One hot afternoon by the tarn, our walk was interrupted by the splash of water dropping from oars, then a call from a rowing boat in which sat the wife and daughters of Henry Disney, warden of the Field Centre.

They recognized Helen, known to them through her many visits to her old haunts, and invited her to join them for tea at the Centre. Without a word to me, or a backward glance, the dumpy little figure scrambled aboard and was rowed away. I

Fn1. reckan-crook: a flat steel bar with a hook at each end, one hook being fixed to a bracket above the fire while a kettle hung from the other.

walked round by the lane and found her seated at the long kitchen table, beaming as she consumed buns and jam tarts as she must have seen the cook and housemaids do during the days long gone when Miss Lodge, Walter Morrison's 'lady' housekeeper, presided. Helen had entered into the very heart of the place which she had, in childhood, regarded with an enormous sense of awe and curiosity. Malham Tarn House had been a place known only to a privileged few.

During Helen's youth, before the First World War, Walter Morrison regularly entertained summer visitors, always including the Reverend Freshfield, his wife and daughters. On Sunday evenings everyone from the scattered community on Malham Moor was welcome to attend areligious service held in the billiard room which led off the Hall's black and white tiled entrance lobby. At that time, a harmonium held pride of place here, as it did in most front parlours on Malham Moor, the instrument being associated with the joy and comfort of singing familiar hymns on Sunday afternoons and evenings. And so it was at the Hall, when Mrs. Freshfield played for the service conducted by her husband, while their daughters played their violins. These occasions allowed families, who met infrequently in less clement seasons, to socialise with their neighbours and provided rare opportunities for the girls to wear hair ribbons and the men a flower in their buttonholes. Before they set off to walk along the track to the Hall, my grandmother, Betty Chester, always picked a rose from the small garden beside the front door of Low Trenhouse, and pinned it to the lapel of my grandfather's jacket.

In later years, Helen recalled how:

"Each summer, Mrs Freshfield would call to see my Mother, bringing with her a lovely parcel of outgrown clothes for our girls. There would usually be a few pairs of long woolly stockings, especially meant to warm little legs during those long cold winters which she knew nowt about."

Helen had duties, even as a small child:

"I was the one who carried up the milk in cans from the farm to the Hall every morning. Miss Lodge always poured me a glass before I left, and Mother said that it gave me my rosy cheeks, and that I was stronger than her other children because of this."

Mr. Battersby, was the coachman, a bachelor who lived above the stables. He was vividly described as *'very well turned out'*, with gaiters so highly polished Helen could see her reflection in them. However, she regarded him with sceptical eyes:

"He didn't have much patience with our boys; for instance, although he would entice them along to give his horses a juicy apple, in return he would only give them one that was sour and woody. They soon learnt not to hang around the yard looking for favours."

Helen's natural curiosity led her to notice much of the minutiae of estate life. She told how Greenwood the gardener mowed the lawns in front of the house with a machine pulled by a little pony called Happy Jack, who wore soft leather boots to protect the turf. In 1927, when the contents of the house were sold 'a set of pony harness and a set of lawn boots' were featured as Lot 507: By this time, six years after the death of Walter Morrison in 1921, the lawns had been untended for many seasons and black rabbits had found favourable grazing on the sweet green slopes between the tarn and the silent, shuttered house. Helen felt sure these rabbits were the progeny of a distinctive strain deliberately introduced by her father so as to help distinguish them from any wild brown rabbits found in poachers' bags. It was typical that she should know exactly where the pony was buried in the tarn woods, alongside the big cart-horses whose lives had also been spent working the estate. Here, too, were buried the crates of yellow china thrown out in 1886, after Morrison, who had represented Plymouth for the Liberal party until 1880, became a bitter opponent of Gladstone's policy for Home Rule in Ireland. His views were strong enough for him to change his political allegiance from the Liberal to the Tory party – after this, all the crockery was blue.

As the years went by, Helen wrote with great feeling for the increasing age and infirmities of her family's revered landlord:

> *'When my brother was a soldier over there,*
> *A millionaire sat in my grandad's chair;*
> *he wouldn't let us help him.*
> *He was an old man, and quite heavy to heave-up out of a chair.*
> *My house is small – no mansion for a millionaire.*
> *But there is room, and room for love and friends.*
> *That's all I care.'*

Helen's working life was spent in service, starting at Skellands, a farm near Malham, where the first verse of 'Down on the Farm' might have been written:

> *'Will... thee git that muck spread*
> *Jane... thee bake t'bread*
> *John... tek yon sour out a t'tank*
> *It's time it were in't fields*
> *As I cam by, it fairly stank'*

Later, at Rylstone House, she kept what may have been her first diary. In this, now lodged with the Yorkshire Archaeological Society, she recorded some of the daily events in and around the household. Surely her cry about plucking ducks which had *'both coats and vest / feathers and down, and made me sob'* came from the heart of a woman who was a hard working keeper's daughter and a housemaid.

Between 1949 and 1960 Arthur Raistrick held courses at the Field Centre in Malham Tarn House, studying and recording prehistoric sites and artefacts on Malham Moor. His lectures for the Workers' Educational Association and the publication of his findings shone a new light on Helen's familiar world. For instance, it must have been a revelation for her to discover the true significance of the tiny, finely fashioned stone tools which lay scattered all around a field near her home. This was later recognized as an important site where Mesolithic hunter-gatherers had spent their summers several thousand years before the Ward children played on those grassy mounds.

Helen became a valued member of Dr Raistrick's 'gang of six' local students, walking the hills and dales in search of the ancient history they could reveal. He appreciated all she could tell him about the places she knew so well, her unerring eye leading her to pick out all manner of things which pointed to the presence of early man. These artefacts might otherwise have lain unrecorded on the surface of the terrain he and his students covered during those heady days.

My last memories of Helen are as a fellow member of the Upper Wharfedale Field Society. She invariably brought something to show during the evening meetings. On one occasion, after she and I had picked up a dead bird on the road near Buckden, she whipped it out of her capacious canvas bag for she had instantly recognized it as a rare green sandpiper. There was no question of simply reporting a sighting; she had so much to say and share with us all.

Helen never married. In the 1940s her sister Gladys became terminally ill and so Helen, in order to nurse her at home, moved into the Hetton cottage where Gladys and her husband Gilbert Stoney lived.

After her sister's death, she stayed on as Gilbert's housekeeper until she herself became infirm and was taken into care in Eshton Hall Nursing Home. There she continued to live life as cheerfully as she could, waited on, with breakfast in bed for the first time in her life. She was surrounded by her plants, and her jottings and drawings, taking pleasure in the many memories her visitors shared with her.

Helen Ward died one early spring day, April 3rd 1988, and was interred in Rylstone churchyard near to the sights and sounds she had loved all her life: lapwings tumbling in flight over their nests in the pastures surrounding the church, while curlews called as they coasted on the wind blowing over the Fell.

Sources:

Hartley, Marie and Ingleby, Joan (1968) Life and Tradition in the Yorkshire Dales p.3, London: J M Dent and Sons Ltd

Raistrick, Arthur (1947) Malham and Malham Moor, Clapham, North Yorkshire: Dalesman Publishing Company Limited

Raistrick, Arthur and Holmes Paul F (1962) Archaeology of Malham Moor, offprint from Field Studies Vol. 1 No 4

Williams, D J and Richardson, J A and R.S, (1987) Mesolithic Sites at Malham Tarn and Great Close Mire, Proceedings of the Prehistoric Society Vol. 53. pp. 363-383.

3. Helen Ward As Others Saw Her

It is worth recognizing this quietly stalwart Daleswoman. Helen Ward lived through times of harshness and hardship but from her early years she absorbed and valued life within her reach. Her beloved Dales presented a rich history and natural beauty which she recorded in paintings and spontaneous poems detailing everyday observations and childhood memories, while her diaries covered a working life in service in several local residences. Some of her notebooks are deposited with the Yorkshire Archaeological Society in Leeds. Helen's practical pursuit of natural history developed her enviable local knowledge and gained her the respect and admiration of local historian Arthur Raistrick.

Phyllida Oates

I first met Helen Ward at Dr Arthur Raistrick's classes on local archaeology for the Workers' Educational Association in the early 1960s. She was the most knowledgeable member of the class, a true Daleswoman with abundant knowledge of country lore and a keen enquiring mind. Later she also attended one of Dr Raistrick's Archaeology courses at Malham Tarn Field Centre and led the group to many otherwise unrecorded sites – lead and coal mines, quarries, archaeological sites, mills, bridges and lime kilns. She frequently picked up bits and pieces for his inspection, not always successfully; one of her finds was summarily dismissed as 'Nay, Helen, it's a bit of nowt.' One of the poems from her collection Small Wonders is dedicated to him:

To a Lecturer

'From Ferrocrete to Malachite
Of these we learnt
By day or night
When out a walk
Or Class attend
When you gave a talk.
When Ancient Walls, thrown on the screen
We saw lots of places, we'd never been.

If you hadn't bothered, we'd never have known
Of fields that were ploughed, and how grew corn.
Of Querns that were broken
And Taxes and such
And how they built houses
Of Thatch and of Crutch

She also joined the Upper Wharfedale Field Society and was especially valued on 'Bring and Show' evenings when she never failed to produce some unusual artefact. The Society made her a Life Member in 1985. Helen Ward worked in several of the larger houses in the district: Rylstone, The Fleets and Netherside Hall, before settling in Hetton. Finally, at Eshton Hall, she tended patches of garden and was allocated a special corner of the entrance hall to keep books, diaries and paintings. Later, a corner with a bay window was partitioned off to provide a private place for her, in which she painted, wrote and knitted for refugee children. She was unique, and a true Daleswoman.

Jean Reinsch

When I knew her, Helen and her brother-in-law Gilbert Stoney lived in the cottage next door but one to the Angel Inn, in Hetton. Gilbert was a good gardener and grew all their vegetables; he had an adjoining cottage which was used to store the gardening tools. Helen kept the garden at the front, full of old fashioned flowers, often sheltering her grey cat and kittens. She knew the names of all the trees, plants, and birds and much local history. She was often to be seen out walking, navy beret pulled straight down Benny Hill style, binoculars slung round her neck, carrying a scrap of paper and a stub of pencil to record anything of interest. She was not afraid of speaking out. One evening, when the chat at a village meeting went on and on, she became impatient and called out "There's Jimmy Saville on the telly and we want to go home to watch him." On her square kitchen table was a plate of moss into which she stuck flower heads or catkins, according to the season, to make an indoor garden.

In the corner by the chest of drawers, there was another garden; a rockery with plants placed among large pebbles. The floor of her kitchen was flagged and partly covered by several large rag rugs. The cottage living room was dominated by a kitchen range with a kettle on a chain over a bright fire, and here we had many cups of smoky tea. I remember Helen Ward as a great storyteller. After our shopping trips to Skipton she and I would sit by the kitchen range while she read her poems or told stories - she had lots to tell, and often spoke about her childhood. For instance, her mother's treat was to stay in bed until the children had gone to school; the eldest girl's job was to dress the younger ones and give them breakfast while her brother Jimmy looked to the dogs. Her mother never discovered that it was actually Helen who fed and exercised the dogs while Jimmy looked to the children. She was a real character.

Margery Budd

4. Winter In Hetton 1947
Excerpts from Helen Ward's Diary

February 10th – Monday

We have not had a daily paper since Monday 3rd. Somebody brought letters twice. Bread and meat and telephone vans came up on Friday when they got cut through but now they are stuck near Scale house on their way back and nowt can get up or down with the new snow. Today the farmers have made another effort and I keep seeing different ones go past on their way to Flasby, where the milk is taken from by wagon.

The birds eat all before them and my word they are thirsty. Gilbert says the Fieldfares have been and eaten up all the Holly berries. Now they are attacking Mr. Snowden's turnips. Mr. Standeven died on Saturday at 3-something.

February 11th – Tuesday Dinnertime

Annie Andrews says young Sills was brought (in) by the snow cutters; he was nearly done for, very cold and tired. He's only 12 and very frail but will go with the men. She had to revive him and put him to lay down a bit.

February 12th – Wednesday

The icicles on Reeday's barn are about 5 or 6 feet long; some as thick as your arm. I've been doing upstairs with a helmet and gloves on. The men are still trying to get the Rylstone/Grassington/Gargrave road open enough for traffic, but they don't know where to put the snow. They are through to Hetton and to Rylstone from Grassington so there are a lot of cutters between Snowden's and the bridge now. Telephones have been working funny: sometimes folks could get through and sometimes they couldn't.

Tommy Shuttleworth gone on with empty horse and float at a tidy pace. 10 to 4 - Milk wagon came up from Gargrave – and Willie Verity after it, then Tommy Shuttleworth, Windle's lorry, 2 Royal Mails, W.R.A.E.C. van, posh black motor, yeast van, little black van, small army wagon, L.M.S. wagon, B.P. petrol wagon, fellows smiling again, private motor car, van, paraffin, meat wagon, L.M.S. full bags, Clayton's, another carry van, Counter's wagon, Stockdale, Helm, all in convoy. Hearse came, turned round at the pub and went away again. Police Sergeant.

It is raw and cold today. It's like a Gala day after all the quiet. A fog is creeping down off the fell. The Sergeant and the Bobby are patrolling Hetton: we couldn't be more honoured if the King was coming.

February 13th – Thursday

It is an offence to use Electric for domestic use from 9 a.m. this morning. Continuing cold for awhile yet… blue van, a lorry load of German prisoners, and a milk wagon gone up. Bobby running, man running – to keep warm I expect. Sergeant smoking a cigarette; takes himself back to the Angel. Snow plough is working again. Mr. Standeven's coffin has been dragged so far by horse and sledge. Old Joe took Jack Taylor's horse sledge.

February 14th – Friday

Philip (a fireman on the railway)… nearly overblown in Bleamoor tunnel. Gilbert says the dog pinched butter ration… and took it into the kennel. It had eaten the butter. Yesterday those eight poor fellows who were trying to get some food to the folks in Staffordshire were killed in the plane crash. Mrs Walker told me yesterday that folks at Burnsall were without food and they were not dug out yet. 1.25 – Mrs Walker had a ring through from the police to say stop all traffic going towards Gargrave as the Fire Engine was coming through to a fire at Burnsall. But one of Stockdale's men says it can't get within four miles of Burnsall, so they look like being burnt out whoever it is. Now Keighley Bobby has rung up to say Keighley Fire Brigade are coming and will she stop all traffic going towards Gargrave, 15 minutes to 2. Now a fire brigade brake has come from Skipton, with two men in it… there is an old pig in the road - it will have to mind its P's and Q's. It's tried snowing a bit today, like sago. It is terribly cold; much colder than yesterday. It is such a biting wind. My Hyacinth is a grand one; it has five heads of flowers out and three more to come out. The cactus is doing well. 4 p.m. - I've just come back from Rylstone and the snowdrifts are immense with what's piled up from the cutting. It's the size of a house and it is just like going into a store. By, that blue look has come into the sky again. We've had it before the other lots of snow. I saw… Myers going to the vault with a wreath. He says Mrs Standeven is very worried and Dennis was paying the fellows overtime to get the road cut open from there to church for the funeral tomorrow.

February 15th – Saturday

Mr. Standeven's funeral. The train got as far as Rylstone. The sun came out quite a few times. Gilbert says he never saw so much snow on the fell and he is turned 40. There seem to be various methods of getting the milk kits back home.

February 16th – Sunday

The sun is shining. I don't think it is as cold, but it seems dryer. There is an awful lot of Gerrys going up. I do hope they work. There is a lot of snow to cut yet. Gilbert says he saw a Gerry going to Snowdens for tea. 60 Gerries were cutting near the station.

February 17th – Monday

It is still as cold as ever. Trying to snow again, but not doing so much. Mrs Walker landed back at noon. She had been to see her Annie who had been found by a neighbour lying on the floor. They thought she must have been there a few hours. She was very cold. Walter said he had been away up Rylstone Fell at the weekend for two sheep and a tup, and they were fair matted up with ice and snow. He said it isn't wise to knock too much off them at once as they feel the cold too much. (Much better to let it thaw off.)

February 18th – Tuesday

A terrible biting wind today, but fine and the sun is shining. I went to Cracoe by the station way, and it is not cut at all in that road. Big drifts from Fleets Road end to Wellocks barn, but I could walk on the drifts and it seemed fairly solid. I saw Mrs Leathley about our dance, and I called to see Mrs. Myers and to leave her a button belonging to her husband's post clothes. She said she was OK. Myers had gone to Bordley last Friday, and it had nearly killed him, she said. The train was just going back to Skipton; no snow cutters had got through to Grassington. The engine had 'Old Faithful' written in chalk across the front. I expect the engine men had done it.

February 19th – Wednesday

The owl over at Rylstone was caught yesterday when it bumped itself into a window. Gilbert said he had hold of it and it was terribly light, but it flew away all right when he held it up.

February 23rd – Sunday

I went to Cracoe… I had to wear my dark glasses; the snow was most dazzling. It was a lovely walk, but very narrow between piles of snow; wall-top high all the way from Cracoe to top of Rectory Hill, which had an immense drift with 'ERIC' printed on it.

February 26th – Wednesday

I've seen no one taking their milk this morning. The snow is coming from the South West this time the 'Bull Noser' as Carr calls it, landed to Rylstone from Skipton.

February 27th – Thursday

I did laugh! I had given the birds some bits and some scraps of cheese. A Bluetit just sat its behind on the snow and held the cheese in its foot. It must have got tired of standing. Next day it was doing it again, and another came and took hold of the other side. In the afternoon I went… to Stainforth to nurse mother who had an awful pain after she got the coals in. And Barbara's feet were a terrible mess. She had great blisters on them, but these we dried up with calamine lotion. It took about eight weeks. I'm sorry to say I haven't the records at the last part of the storm as all my time was taken up nursing. When the snow went it was a lovely spring and things soon seemed to be a lovely green.

Source

Excerpts from her Hetton diaries, recalling the memorable winter storm of 1947, form part of the UWFS archives. They were originally recorded on tape by Robert Chisholm, past President of the UWFS.

Thorpe Cave, Elbolton
From: John Crowther's 'Walks Around Grassington' 1920

5. Barden, an Estate Township

Heather Beaumont

There is no village at Barden in Upper Wharfedale. The ruins of Barden Tower provide a topographical focus for the township, and also a key to its history. From the Norman Conquest to the present day Barden has been owned by the nobility, and through 900 years of history it has evolved from a medieval hunting chase into an agricultural and sporting estate. The area includes some of the most beautiful stretches of the river Wharfe; today these are bordered by woodland and pasture and dotted with isolated farms and small hamlets. To the west the land rises steeply to the heather-clad heights of Barden Moor with Simon's Seat and Barden Fell to the north and east.

The Forest of Barden was amongst the possessions of the Honour of Skipton granted in 1066 to Robert de Romille by William I. In 1155 Alice de Romille provided the Augustinian Canons of Embsay with a site for their new priory at Bolton, on the southern edge of the forest.

By 1310, when Robert Clifford became Lord of the Honour of Skipton, Barden was a hunting forest, with six forest lodges. The names and sites of the lodges have been perpetuated. They include Barden Tower itself, the hamlets of Drebley and Howgill and the farmsteads of Laund and Gamsworth. The site of the sixth lodge, Ungaine, remains in name only, as land near Bolton Priory.

Unlike the royal forests, those held from the sovereign by noble subjects were areas in which game such as deer and wild boar were conserved as a valuable food resource. In this context, the term 'forest' refers to an area having its own officials, laws and courts, which were administered to safeguard its resources. These included game, grazing and forage, minerals, peat for fuel, and natural products such as honey and wax, as well as timber for building and a multiplicity of other purposes, including bark for tanning. Not all hunting forests were wooded.

Barden, however, was renowned for its trees and timber; the fine oaks that remain are doubtless the progeny of ancient stock. Holly trees, particularly numerous beside the road that links Barden with Hazlewood and Storiths, are a reminder that clippings from the upper, smooth-leaved branches were fed to deer and domestic stock as winter fodder or 'husset'. Barden Tower became the principal lodge and the venue for the forest courts. It was developed as a manorial centre by Henry Clifford, tenth Lord of the Honour of Skipton, known as "The Shepherd Lord".

He built the core of the stone, keep-like structure, about 1484, and later, between 1516 and 1517, a separate chapel to the south of the tower precinct. He is reputed to have preferred his Barden residence to Skipton castle. In an area liable to raids by the Scots, its defensible position was advantageous. Although not on a hill top, the tower is at a good vantage-point and commands the river crossing where the valley narrows.

Fig. 15. Barden Tower, the Chapel and bridge over the River Wharfe (courtesy of R.White.YDNP)

Many features associated with the Tower are typical of a medieval manor. They include Little Park, where earth works remains to the south of the Tower suggest gardens, and a group of medieval barns and fishponds beyond, with a walled, funnel-shaped access to what was originally unenclosed pasture. There is also a coney warren, marked on current Ordnance Survey maps; its long, curving wall can be seen from the roadside near Barden Scale. Extending westward from the Tower across Barden Moor, and now enclosing Lower Barden reservoir, an extensive enclosure formed the deer park, named Great or Broad Park.

The river crossing, now Barden Bridge, provides a link between different parts of the township. If the bridge is represented by the crosspiece of the letter H, (Fig 15) the township extended as four limbs on the east and west banks of the river, upstream and downstream. Thus the area around the tower was the site of 'public buildings', reasonably accessible to all residents: first, the forest court and a school, later Anglican and Wesleyan chapels, and an inn which in the era of Victorian self-improvement became a reading room. The bridge also carried a road link between Skipton and Pateley Bridge, via Howgill and Skyreholme, possibly a route for lead mined at Greenhow and Appletreewick. By the 17th century, the economy of the forest was undergoing a change, as the inhabitants began to practise agriculture and became rent-payers. The terms of the leases granted by the Cliffords to their tenants in Barden between 1602 and 1605 show what life must have been like for farmers living within a hunting forest, where the interests of the landowner remained paramount.

Tenants had to undertake 'to be of good behaviour towards the deer and game'. They also had to assist in the maintenance of the forest, by planting 'five young trees of oak, ash, or elm, yearly on the premises'. One tenant was additionally instructed 'from time to time to do his best to endeavour to preserve and maintain the said trees from wind and weather and from the spoil of cattle'. Those granted grazing rights in Barden Great Park had to allow 'liberty for the deer and game to feed on the premises, and liberty for the officers and keepers of the Earl to walk and run over the premises for viewing, chasing, driving of the deer that may come thereon.' Cottagers were granted common rights. Thus in 1650, Lady Anne Clifford, Countess Dowager of Pembroke granted to Ellen Atkinson of Gillbeck and to Antonie Bounbie of Holehouse rights of 'pasture, turbary, i.e. to dig peat, and liberty to grave, get and carry away turfs, sods, stones, ling, bracken, rushes, and thatch throughout all the outmoors, commons and wastes belonging to Barden west side according to the ancient yearly rent of 16d' (6½p). [1]

Tenants named Atkinson farmed near Gillbeck, at Low House and Club Nook, for about 300 years, and the Demaine family were at Barden Scale and Drebley for a similar period. Other families with long tenancies in Barden include Holmes, Inman, Ideson, Lister, Thompson, and Ward. [2 & 3] In addition to the names of the forest lodges in the 17th century leases, [4] there are references to other farms, the names of which have persisted to the present day, such as Woodend, Eastwood Head, Broadshaw.

A few field names have also survived, while Hough Mill at Howgill has a long history as the soke mill of Barden.

Traditionally, buildings in Barden were constructed around large 'A' shaped wooden crucks and trusses which supported steeply pitched roofs thatched with heather, or ling. A few cruck buildings remain to this day, testifying to the durability of the large timbers derived from the oaks which thrive on the gritstone soil of Barden. Later buildings had higher walls with stone slated roofs of shallow pitch, and many farmhouses and barns were extensively repaired or re-built during the 19th century. [5]

Walled enclosures developed gradually. Some of the longest and earliest probably surrounded deer parks and took the form of embankments surrounded by palings or walls. Broad Park had been enclosed by the first half of the 17th century, as had a large enclosure known as Drebley Thwaite. [6] The earliest field walls were built in proximity to farmsteads, as shown on the 1731 map; [7] many of these can be identified today. The creation of small 'intakes' and enclosures from woodland and rough pasture is further evidence of the movement away from the management of game towards the improvement of the land and more efficient agriculture. Small acreages were devoted to arable crops before better transport allowed corn and flour to be brought in. As dictated by climate and terrain, stock rearing has long been the primary occupation in Barden. Cattle and sheep, many of them originating from Scotland, were grazed, and sold at the great fairs, such as the one held each October at Great Close on Malham Moor. They were overwintered in Craven, fattened during the summer, and sold for meat in the autumn.

During the late 18th and 19th centuries demand increased as industrial centres in West Yorkshire and Lancashire developed. Agricultural improvement continued during the early years of the 19th century, by which time the enclosures had been completed.

Drebley Thwaite was sub-divided in 1812, [8] creating a length of road between Barden and Burnsall, now the B6160. At this time, also, woodland which had previously been leased at low rentals for pasture, was 'taken in hand' to be managed by the estate. 9 In addition, the pendulum swung in favour of the management of game, particularly grouse, on the wide expanses of heather moorland, while the beauty of the area began to be developed and exploited as a tourist attraction. Many features from the past survive in the present landscape, and can be seen from public roads and footpaths, such as the riverside track between Hough Mill and Barden Bridge, or the track from Howgill to the summit of Simon's Seat.

Acknowledgements

With thanks to Peter Watkins, archivist at Bolton Abbey, and the Trustees of the Chatsworth Settlement, to Dr. Richard Spence, and to Robert White for permission to print the aerial photograph of Barden Tower and its precincts.

1 Skipton MSS, Yorkshire Archaeological Society, Leeds (YAS). DD 187/7: Barden leases 1602-57 (abstracts made by WE Preston, 1953-4). DD 121/24/4: Books of grants of land in Craven, Barden 1650-55. DD 121/25/29, 35, 36: Barden rentals 1603, 1654, 1655

2 Skipton MSS: 32 Bolton MSS: Barden Township: Chatsworth collection

3 Bolton MSS: Rentals, eg 1687, 1698, 1754/5, 1776, 1785

4 Bolton MSS: Surveys, valuations and rentals, eg 1806/7, 1867

5 Bolton MSS

6 Bolton MSS: Estate maps: 1730 (copies dated 1731 and 1788), 1806, 1867

7 Bolton MSS: division of Drebley Thwaite, 1812

8 Bolton MSS.

6. Two Villages: Conistone with Kilnsey

Jacqueline Keighley

The road up-dale leading from Threshfield to Kettlewell passes through the woodlands of Netherside and Long Ashes until it reaches Kirk Bank. From here, a splendid view of the River Wharfe takes in the villages of Conistone and Kilnsey. Divided by the river, Conistone lies on the east side and Kilnsey on the west; two separate entities from the beginning. They have, however, much in common through their geology and geography, and they owe their existence to the river and the valley.

In the last Ice Age the area was covered with ice. As the glacier moved south it gorged away a limestone cliff, leaving a U-shaped valley through which the river now flows, and Kilnsey Crag with the overhang that we see today. As the glacier came and went, debris collected, and formed a moraine on which much of the village of Kilnsey is built.

Beneath this deposit is the Great Scar Limestone. The glacier's terminal moraine is at Mill Scar Lash, and this originally formed a barrier across the valley floor, forming a great lake of melt water. Later the river cut through, but we are reminded of the lake when the river is in flood today and separates the two villages.

The village of Conistone (Fig. 16.) faces south-west whereas Kilnsey faces east. This situation, together with the position of the background hills, means that at certain times of the year Conistone has four more hours of sunshine a day than Kilnsey. This makes arable farming on the Conistone side of the valley more viable. Geologically, Conistone has a bonus too, for although the lower part of the village is on limestone and has a glorious limestone flora, the scenery changes as you climb eastwards.

At about 1200 ft., white limestone gives way to grey millstone grit supporting peat bogs and heather moorland. In the past, peat was the main source of fuel, and heather has always been food for grouse. In Kilnsey even the highest ground is limestone and here the rare bird's eye primrose can occasionally be found. Because limestone is porous, streams are constantly changing their courses; in Conistone most of the streams are underground – Girling Trough is now completely dry but probably brought water to Conistone at one time. In Kilnsey there is much more surface water, especially below the Crag at Northcote, as well as in Sikes Beck and in Howgill, both draining into White Beck and thence to the river.

The remains of ancient settlements can be seen on both sides of the valley, high up on the limestone terraces, well away from floods. There is some evidence of Bronze Age occupation and in the Iron Age (approximately 500BC-500AD) there appears to have been a sizeable population in both villages. Many old enclosures can be seen on High Castles Scar and Swineber Scar in Conistone, and in Kilnsey along Mastiles Lane and above Chapel House wood. The Romans may have had a route through the villages but there is no evidence of Roman settlement.

The Angles from North Germany invaded England in the 5th century, settled in East Yorkshire, and then made their way westwards; the suffix 'tun' in place names such as Conistone is evidence of their arrival.

Fig. 16. The Village of Conistone, (Thomas Ryder, 'Rambles' p45)

King Edwin established Christianity in the north soon after 625AD, but the oldest part of the present Conistone church is thought to date from the early part of the 11th century it cannot be certain whether there was a church here as early as the first Anglian settlement. Arthur Raistrick considered the present church to be in its original position together with the burial ground, outside the village.

Anglian cultivation terraces surround Conistone village. These are known as lynchets, and show up clearly when there is a powdering of snow. There were common fields for arable use, common pasture and meadow, and a droveway across the arable fields to the pasture, possibly the present day track from Pasture Gate.

35

The pound, where stray cattle were held, has survived as a small enclosure in the centre of the village.

Access roads led from the village across the arable fields and where these ancient roads linked one village to the next, they frequently deviated around boundaries of natural features. A splendid example can still be seen in the double right angled bend in Conistone 'back road' at Whitey Nook, marking the medieval boundary between Grassington and Conistone.

No bridge is recorded in Conistone before 1175 when it would have been built of wood and been vulnerable during flooding.

Fig. 17. Kilnsey reflected in the modern Trout Hatchery. Photo: Jane Hargreaves

The Angles do not appear to have settled in Kilnsey. In the 10th Century Norse invaders came from north-west Norway by way of Shetland, Orkney, and Northern Ireland, landed on the north-west coast of England and gradually made their way through Lancashire towards Yorkshire, probably approaching Wharfedale by the route which became known as Mastiles Lane. They preferred high fell lands and steep valley heads and so settled on high ground around Kilnsey, forming a scattered community of farmsteads spreading west across the high fells to Malham. The sites of Trenhouse and Middle House were two of these 71 outlying farms. The Norse 'hus' usually consisted of one or two houses occupied by fathers and their sons, with a few adjacent crofts and meadows surrounded by a wide area of upland pasture. Sheep farming was the main occupation but they also kept cattle and pigs. Chapel House farm forms the southern boundary of Kilnsey, while the medieval site of Northcote, which is still a farm, lies on the northern boundary (Fig. 17).

Before the Norman Conquest Kilnsey had been in the hands of a Saxon thane named Gamel. Norman barons generally replaced the Saxon overlords, eventually becoming dukes, but in Kilnsey, as in other remote places regarded by William the Conqueror as 'wasteland', the Saxon thane survived.

At the time of the Domesday survey in 1086, Conistone was a single manor. In 1100 William II granted Conistone with Kilnsey, Rylstone, Burnsall and Bordley to the de Romille family who held it until 1156.

Conistone then passed to the de Hebden family, who held it for most of the monastic period. Monastic records show a house and pasture for 500 sheep, which could have been Gill House, up on the moor towards Mossdale or Gill House Beck, with access to Nidderdale and so to the Abbey at Fountains.

Alice de Romille granted the manor of Kilnsey and the adjoining lands to the recently founded Fountains Abbey and for nearly 400 years the monks of Fountains held this vast estate; they brought prosperity and imposed a new pattern on the countryside. During the monastic period, sheep farming was highly organised, there being a grange at Kilnsey, which was the local administrative centre. [Fn1]

The foundations of a medieval sheep house can be seen below Hill Castle Scar and may be similar to the one which belonged to Bolton Priory on Malham Moor.

This could have been the centre of an extensive system of enclosures built for handling the animals of Fountains Abbey. The monastic buildings included a dwelling house with a hall, a courthouse for settling differences, storehouses, great barns, and a chapel. The earliest of these buildings were of timber with wattle and daub infill, thatched with rushes grown by the river. Further afield, there were eight scattered principal houses with barns for storage, and also a corn mill and a fulling mill near Mill Scar Lash. Late in the 15th Century these monastic buildings were rebuilt in stone and enclosed by a stone wall. The gatehouse was built about this time, and part of it has survived in the precincts of the Old Hall. (Fig. 18)

In the Middle Ages, Kilnsey Moor seems to have been seriously overstocked with sheep. The animals were not kept as a source of meat, since wool production was the main object of the farming, but the ewes were milked and cheese and butter were sentto the abbey.

The cellarer and other lay brothers kept the accounts and manned the grange, but

---

Fn1. Grange: an outlying farmhouse with barns for storing tithes, belonging to a monastery or feudal lord. Most had a chapel, and some had special products, e.g. Kilnsey produced wool and thatching reeds.

work on the farms was done entirely by local tenant farmers. Shepherding on open moorland was a hard task, for the sheepfolds were far away from human habitation, and shepherds lived in huts on the moor.

Monks from Fountains visited Kilnsey regularly to say Mass, and, on rare occasions the Abbot came. His visits were great events, with much celebration.

Chapel House at Kilnsey is first mentioned in Monastic Records, and is listed with the scattered Norse farms. By the 15th Century, owned by the Yorkes, it was a centre for rearing young lambs, with Robert and John Layland as tenant farmers. By 1539, the date of the Dissolution, the abbey's finances had been declining for some time and much of the business was already in the hands of laymen, who continued to act for the tenants, but the cessation of the abbey wool trade does not seem to have caused a tremendous upheaval in Kilnsey.

Fig. 18. Kilnsey Old Hall
and the remains of the 15th century gatehouse.
by Julian Anderson B.A. (Hons.) Fine Art

In 1571 the holdings were offered to sitting tenants. About this time two brothers named Wade came to Kilnsey from Addingham, married into local families and acquired local farms. In the next generation, Christopher Wade inherited the property at the age of 22, and immediately set about improving the land and enlarging the estate; by the time he was middle aged he had bought three more farms and set himself up as squire of the village. In 1648 he built Kilnsey Old Hall (see Fig. 18), using ready dressed stone from the old monastic buildings. His son Cuthbert succeeded him and again, during his lifetime, the Kilnsey estate grew and flourished. Lady Anne Clifford stayed twice at the Hall as Cuthbert's guest, once in 1663, and again in 1666. After the Wade family died out; the Hall was let to tenants but by 1800 it was being used as a barn, and remained so for nearly two hundred years.

We know very little about Conistone in the monastic period, but below Swineber Scar a medieval house survives, with fine stone shelves. The manor remained with the de Hebdens until the middle of the 16th Century. By 1583 it was in the hands of John Kaye of Oakenshaw, who disposed of it in such a way that the history of Conistone was completely changed for the next 300 years. Kaye sold Conistone to 27 separate people, 13 of whom were sitting tenants; the other 14 did not live within the manor but acted as trustees. The list of their names implies that most were either related to the tenants, or had some other interest in the land, perhaps already working on it. These 27 people became freeholders who not only owned their own farms, but they also shared joint ownership of the moor and commons, with all rights appertaining to them: the rights of turbary (cutting peat) and estovers (collecting wood), the shooting rights and, later, the mineral rights. They had responsibilities for the upkeep of roads and fences, and the provision and upkeep of the pound for stray cattle, under joint control of the parish. Provision was also made for shelter and food for tramps passing through the village. Each year one of the freeholders was appointed Bylawman who chose four others to assist him. For over three centuries this was the pattern of village rule, keeping the peace between owners and occupiers of land, publishing bylaws and demanding fines from those who did not obey them. If fines were unpaid the culprits were referred to the Council of the North and doubtless imprisonment or even worse followed. The Bylawman set the stint of pastures [Fn1] and let the shooting. One of the Bylawman's tasks was to 'drive the pastures' from time to time, gathering up the animals, counting them and making lists of all gate-holders [Fn2] and their sheep, cattle and horses. When Old Pasture became overstocked, other land, higher up the fell, had to be enclosed. Eventually, Old Pasture was kept for cows, Kelber for horses, New Close for sheep, and Nook took the overflow.

In the 17th Century veins of lead were found on the edge of Conistone moor near Mossdale. The Bylawman then appointed a Barmaster who issued licences and regulated the mines. Although Royalties were paid to the freeholders it was never a very profitable venture and was mostly done part-time, by local people.

In Kilnsey lead-mining was even more primitive; there are the remains of many bell pits scattered over the moor. Many farmers dug a few pits, but with little profitability, and a smelt mill was built in Kilnsey (behind the present fish farm). The smelting process, in the early days, was done in ore hearths, fuel for the process being acquired locally. Initially, charcoal was produced by using seasoned timber, mainly from mature oak and beech trees, with resulting devastation of the forests.

Another fuel, known as 'white coal', consisted of small pieces of saplings obtained by coppicing, and dried so as to drive out all the sap.

Fn1 Stinted pastures: Common land divided into pastures, each allotted to a person allowed to graze a limited number of cattle there.
Fn2 Gateholder: from Old Norse 'gata', cattle walk: the holder of a 'gate', a cattle walk or pasture.

This drying process was carried out in kilns, known as elling hearths, and the remains of these can still be seen in both Conistone and Kilnsey. Each hearth took the form of a bowl-shaped hollow, about 10 feet wide and 7-8 feet deep, lined with boulders, and with a raised dry-stone edge and an entrance or firing-hole sloping down into the bowl. Large branches of wood were laid across the bowl to make a floor, on which the small pieces of wood were arranged in layers. Brushwood and loppings were burned in the bowl beneath, and the heat and smoke from the fire drove out all the sap in the small wood, leaving behind a fuel ideal for smelting, which was 'white coal'. When the elling was complete, the wood ash was raked out from the hearth and was sold to soap and glass makers to be used in their processes. The elling process was very labour-intensive, for the fire had to be constantly watched and regularly fed to ensure that the wood was heated but not burnt.

Elling hearths were in use in the 17th and 18th centuries, until the reverberatory furnace displaced the ore hearth and coal became the general fuel.

There are remains of about 200 elling hearths in Upper Wharfedale.

In the early 18th century the centre of the Kilnsey estate seems to have moved from the Hall to Chapel House, with the Tennant family now at the helm. John Tennant of Bordley had bought Chapel House from the Yorkes in 1572, whilst the Layland family were living there. In 1690 the Laylands left Chapel House and crossed to the sunny side of the valley; Laylands Cottage in Conistone may well have been their 'retirement home'. Documents show that a second John Tennant purchased land from Cuthbert Wade in 1727, and that part of Chapel House was rebuilt in Georgian style shortly before his death in 1790. The Tennant family gradually took over the estate and held it until 1900.

Throughout the 18th century, the allocation of farming land became increasingly difficult and so the freeholders applied to Parliament for permission to divide and enclose the pastures. An Enclosure Award was made in 1801, after which, much of the work of the Bylawman was finished. However, until the formation of the Joint Parish Meeting of Conistone with Kilnsey in 1883, chaired by J. Tennant of Chapel House, the Bylawmen still kept order in the village and its common lands.

Transcribed from Dr. Keighley's Presidential Address to the Upper Wharfedale Field Society 1991.

Sources:
Raistrick, A. (1967) Old Yorkshire Dales Newton Abbot: David and Charles.
Raistrick, A. (1968) The Penine Dales London: Eyre and Spottiswoode.
Michelmore, D.J.H. (1981) The Fountains Abbey Lease Book. Edited for the Yorkshire Archaeological Society Record Series Vol. CXL: Leeds: University Printing Service.
Ashley Cooper, Anne (1988) Yorke Country Luton, Bedfordshire: White Crescent Press Ltd.

7. The Old Coach Road From Skipton To Richmond – Following Ogilby's Map 1765

Helen Lefèvre

The London coach road from Skipton to Richmond via Wharfedale and Coverdale is shown on Ogilby's road map of 1675 [1] (Fig. 19) and was described in 1719 by Thomas Gardiner:

'From Skipton ascend a hill, leave Stirton village on left, cross 3 Brooks and at 224' 3 come to Lord Burlington's Park on the Right, lying on the road for above a mile, over 3 Brooks ascend a hill, pass through Rilstone V. of 3 F and by Crakston on the right. Then over a hill succeeded by two descents, cross a Brook and go by a Lake on the right called the Tarn at 230 M through Linton V. and over a Valley arrive at Rashby V. there crossing Linton Stone Bridge over Wharfe flv. set forward by Grassington V. on the Right, through a large Wood by a hill on left to Coniston V. of near 2 Furlongs at 223' 6. Hence over 3 Brooks and by an Inn on the right, pass at 226' 5 to Kettlewell Village of 2 F where ascending and crossing a valley go through a Park and ascend again. At 239' 6 descend to a Moor and leave Coverdale V. on left descending and ascending pass large Valley in which re seated Woodall, Bradley, Horse House Chapel and Garsgill, all small villages at 246, leaving the Vale enter Carlton V of 4 F whence Coverham flv. runs by the side of the road on right for several miles'. [2]

At 247' 7 pass through Melmerby V. and one mile further on Ocklethorp V. by the seat of the Lord of St John on left, whence a straight road over moor to Midlam or Middleham at 251' 4 of 6 F on the Right seated on Yore flv., having a Market on Mon.

Thence over Yore flv., ascend a hill, pass through Harny V. and over moor, cross several waters. At 255' 7 over hill of 7 F and a valley, and at 258' 7 come to a decent of 10 F at bottom of which cross a brook and leave a Lead House on left. Thence through a valley descend and cross Swale flv. over a stone bridge to Richmond, large and well built having a market on Saturday.' [3]

The road left Skipton by Mill Bridge, went up Raikes Road and turned right down Sod Hill to where the present roundabout is situated. Its line can be traced on the left of the Grassington road near the corner, by a bank and a line of thorn trees. It is now crossed by the present Grassington road (B 6265) and can be traced at intervals by a similar bank.

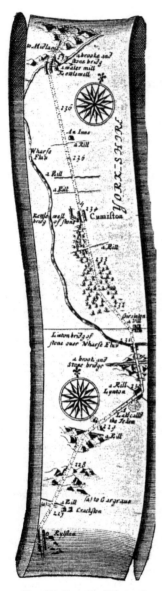

At what is now Sandy Beck Bar the road exists as a clear wide lane (Fig. 18) to the east of the present road, passing over a hill between Scale House and Norton Tower, emerging at Rylstone.

It is known to have passed to the west of the church, and near the old fish ponds it is found as a lane with part wall, part hedge which can be followed as far as Cracoe. Part way along lies the base of the old boundary stone between Cracoe and Rylstone.

Here the lane is marked on ordnance survey maps variously as Chapel Lane or Rectory Lane, as Rylstone church was originally a chapelry in the Parish of Burnsall.

At Cracoe, the path of the old road is lost because the present road was made in the 1760s, but traces of it have been found in a field to the west of the village. It then probably went along the slope of Swindon Hill to avoid the soft ground around the edge of a glacial lake that filled Linton Bottoms; this was not drained until about the middle of the 19th century.

The road is traceable again as Farlands Lane, which drops into Linton. There was no bridge at Linton, so the beck had to be forded. From here, the present road follows the old route to Great Bank Top, (where Ogilby marks a crossroad), down Great Bank, to cross over Bow Bridge and along Falls Road to Linton Bridge (now called Grassington Bridge) where it crosses the Wharfe. The old route missed Grassington village and went north by a bridleway, emerging at the bottom of Bull Ing Lane.

From here, the road passed along Wood Lane and through Grass Wood. It then cut across a field to the corner of the road at White Nook Barn, and followed the line of the present road

Fig. 19. Detail of Map of The Old Coach Road (Ogilby)

as far as Conistone. On this section of road, just beyond the barn there is a hedge which bears every trace of being very old, in that it is composed of many species.

Fig. 20. The Old Coach Road approaching Sandy Beck Bar

About halfway between Conistone and Kettlewell, Ogilby marks an inn, one of the very few to be noted, the site corresponding to the present Mile House Farm. At Kettlewell it crossed the beck by a stone bridge and followed the line of the present road going up a hill, Park Rash, (a park is marked on the map) beyond which it 'enters a Moor'. [4]

The map then shows how the road went down Coverdale to Horse Houses where a chapel is marked, and on through Carlton and Ocklethorpe (now Agglethorpe.) The route from there is difficult to trace, but coaches arrived at Middleham where the Yore was crossed by a ford.

This is not marked on Ogilby's map, but is labelled as such on some other early maps. The rest of the road is difficult to trace - it went through Harmby and Hipswell, now occupied by Catterick Camp, and crossed the Swale over a stone bridge into Richmond.

From Chronicles and Stories of the Yorkshire Dales
J H Dixon

'How did the Skiptonians reach Rylstone? Some went round by Gargrave and Hetton; and others turned off at the top of Skipton Raikes, and passing through Short Lea Lane, managed, by following horse-paths, carried over undrained swampy pastures, (once the bed of a small lake called Alenwath tarn), to reach the road from Embsay to None-go-by. From hence there was a road, principally carried through undrained

43

pastures to Scale House, beyond which the road to Rylstone was plain enough, and followed an ancient Roman via, which, up-hill and downdale, soon brought the weary traveller to the 'towngates of Troy'.

(Traces of the via can be seen immediately beneath Norton Tower, where a causeway, constructed of large blocks of stone, is evidently of Roman workmanship) About 90 years ago this route was improved in two places; for the enclosure of Scale House pastures led to the formation of a road between Sandybeck and the above mentioned Roman road. About the same time a road was constructed, which commenced at None-go-by, and was carried, in a tolerably straight line, past the place where the modern inn The Craven Heifer stands, and so to the old road between Skipton and Gargrave. It was reported that the old Skipton to Rylstone road, even in its improved state, was as vile a piece of civil engineering as ever was constructed. It was badly drained, and when repaired by township benevolence the principal material employed was a soft sandstone.

Some portions of this paragon of a road were carried up inclines, with gradients ranging from one to twelve, to even one in eight. And this was a pass which led to not only the principal and most romantic dales of West Yorkshire, but to the route over which the extensive mineral traffic of Grassington, and the country ten miles beyond it, had to be conveyed.

The new road, after leaving Skipton, winds up a small valley under Park-hill, the sides of which formerly waved with fruit and forest trees ...and so on to Sandybeck, where a tollhouse is erected. (The Trust having expired, the turnpike gate has now been removed, and the house is no longer occupied by a toll collector.) Here commences the most important diversion, for the new road pursues the valley about 20 yards below Scale House, till its termination at Rylstone. The land about is studded with natural wood, and clusters of birch, holly and alder, watered by a fine brook, which takes its name from the alder tree's fine designation, and so is called Ellerbeck.

On one side we have the lofty summits of Crookrise, with their huge masses of grit crags called Brass Castle and Fairies' Chests. Further on is Rylstone Fell, with its brown heath, and the rugged walls of Norton Tower - a conspicuous object to all the surrounding country. On the opposite side of the valley, to which has been given the appropriate name, Ellerdale, are the Flasby Fells. They are not very high; but there is great beauty in their wood-clad summits. The termination of the valley spreads before us, the rich grazing grounds of Rylstone, and the most extensive prospect, extending to Pendle Hill and forest on one side, and the high grounds of Malham moor and Bordley on the other. In the far distance, are the mist-clad mountains of Upper Wharfedale.

Great improvements are in progress along the whole line of the new road that an omnibus travels daily.' [5]

The Toll Bar at Sandybeck
Brontë Bedford-Payne

Ella Pontefract and Marie Hartley recount how the old road remained a green lane after the turnpike was made, farmers and carriers still using it on occasion in order to escape the toll, especially after dark when the tolls were doubled. 'Grassington boys, fetching coal from Skipton, still went that way in their small 'galloway' carts. The journey took them two hours each way transported half a ton, perhaps twenty or thirty per day. A boy got sixpence for the journey and fourpence for his dinner in Skipton, and was given his tea when he got back to Grassington. [6]

Raistrick reminds us that, after the coming of the turnpike road, 'Skipton market took precedence over Pateley and Ripon, the markets at Kettlewell and Grassington ceased and there was a great increase in cattle dealing. Coal, lead, corn and cattle were concentrated at the Skipton wharves on the Leeds and Liverpool canal'. 7

Fig. 21a. Toll Bar

In 2006 the former turnpike road still links Skipton and Rylstone, as part of the B6265.

All that remains of the Toll Bar at Sandybeck are shown in a photographs taken in 1999. Unexpectedly, openings in the wall (21a & 21b) indicate that it fronted the old coach road, suggesting that travellers were directed away from the turnpike to pay their tolls The two openings are one above the other. Was the upper one to enable the coachman to pay his dues without dismounting, and the lower for the use of mounted packmen and foot travellers to pass the time of day as they paid their toll?

Fig. 21b. Interior of Toll Bar showing toll windows

45

From the beginning of the twentieth century the cottage at Sandy Beck Bar (Fig. 21c) was home to the family of Owen Griffiths, coachman and later chauffeur to the Standeven family at Scale House. After he died in 1946, the cottage was left uninhabited, its roofing slates and timbers removed, leaving a rather desolate reminder of a bygone age at this isolated spot.

Fig. 21c. Old Toll Bar Cottage

References

1. 'The continuation of the extended Road from Oakham in Rutland to Richmond com Ebor' A section of the map drawn in 1675 by John Ogilby Esq. His Majesty's Cosmographer.

2. Gardiner, Thomas A Pocket Guide to the English Traveller being a Compleat Survey and Admeasurement of all the Principal Roads and Most Considerable Cross Roads in England and Wales in One Hundred Copper Plates, printed for J.Turner of Shakspear's Head over against Katharine St. in the Strand and J. Walls at the Printing Office in Wild Court near Lincoln's Inn Fields, MDCCXIX.

3. ibid.

4. ibid

5. Dixon, J.H. Chronicles and Stories of the Yorkshire Dales 1881 Chapter IX, pp. 142-149. London: Simpkin Marshall & Co., Skipton: Edmondson & Co.

6. Pontefract, Ella and Hartley, Marie (1938) Wharfedale London: J M Dent & Sons Ltd pp. 164-165.

7. Raistrick, Arthur (1967) Old Yorkshire Dales Devon: David & Charles pp 107-108.

Education

Ted Gower's drawing of Barden School

8. Threshfield School and the Matthew Hewitt Scholars

Turning Sons of Husbandmen into Anglican Clergy

Martha Kneale

I suppose that everyone who has passed Threshfield School (Fig. 22) in Church Road has noticed the lovely building there. Perhaps out of curiosity you have gone up to the front and seen that it is dated 1674 (Fig. 23), and was founded by Matthew Hewitt, Rector of one mediety in the Parish of Linton in Craven (divided, since the 11th century, into two medieties). You may also have seen in Linton church the board which lists the various benefactions made in this Parish (Fig. 24). This records not only Hewitt's foundation of the school, but also the fact that he left £50 a year to support four exhibitioners at St. John's College, Cambridge.

This means that one man went to Cambridge as an exhibitioner every year, four being there at any one time, each supported by £12 10s per annum.

Fig. 22. Threshfield School. (Thomas Ryder, 'Rambles' p36)

Ever since I saw the benefactions board, I have been curious about these exhibitioners. I wanted to know who they were, where they came from, and what happened to them as a result of their move from Threshfield to Cambridge. First I obtained a list of names from the headmaster of Threshfield School. A slightly more extensive list came later from another local source. These I put together and called the Threshfield lists.

Fig. 23. Commemoration Tablet

There is also a Cambridge list, derived from a publication of the last century by Michael Venn, *'Alumni Cantarbrigienses'*. This is an enormous volume containing a history, up to the time when Venn was recording it, of all the graduates of Cambridge University. I also used Thomas Whitaker's *'History and Antiquities of the Deanery of Craven'* third edition, published in 1878, and *'Silva Gars'* written by a local antiquarian, P.J. Crowther, in 1930. This says, inaccurately, of the school building

'This venerable Elizabethan edifice has now passed its 150th birthday...', whereas it is has now passed its 300th birthday, and, if built in 1674 is Jacobean, not Elizabethan. Crowther describes how:

'The most celebrated pupils of this school were Dr. Whitaker, the historian of Craven, Dr. Dodgson, who became Bishop of Elphin, Dr. William Craven, last Master of St. John's College Cambridge, the Reverend William Sheepshanks, Dr. Paley, author of 'Evidences of Christianity', Archdeacon Stackhouse, who wrote a commentary on the bible, the Reverend Bailey J. Harker, a local author and poet; all received the rudiments of education there, and their names surely form a worthy list of learned and honoured men to be connected with the old seminary.' [1]

Whitaker says:

'Matthew Hewitt, Rector of one mediety of Linton,... founded a grammar school at Threshfield, endowing it with £20 per annum for the Master, and £10 for the Usher, and four exhibitions at £12 each to scholars of St John's College in Cambridge, but the great depreciation of money which has taken place in the last century proves the

impolicy of such pensionary endowments, and the school has been so little distinguished, either for able masters or for hopeful scholars, that it has not been unusual in St. John's College to apply to it the text 'out of Galilee ariseth no prophet'. In this opprobrium the author of the 'History of Craven' must be content to partake. Yet a few exceptions might be mentioned. The late Bishop of Elphin, Dr. Dodgson, as well as Dr. William Craven, born at Gouthwaite Hall in Netherdale, the present learned and venerable Master of St. Johns College, were among the number of Hewitt's distinguished exhibitioners.' [2]

However, Venn's Cambridge list differs, saying that the Dodgson who became Bishop of Elphin was not the same Dodgson who was at Threshfield. There were three Dodgsons shown; oddly enough, all their first names began with 'C'.

Now the Dodgson who became Bishop of Elphin was Charles Dodgson – also at St. John's – the Dodgson who was at Threshfield was Christopher, and he ended his life as Vicar of Airmyn, now in East Yorkshire.

But what about William Craven? He didn't occur on either of my Threshfield lists. So was he really at Threshfield School at all? Although he lived in Nidderdale, I had my doubts. A William Craven did go on to St. John's, but from Sedbergh. Did he perhaps come to Threshfield first for a year or two, then to Sedbergh to finish his school education, and from there to St. John's? The fact that he was at Sedbergh is confirmed by the records of Sedbergh School and if this was so, he could not have been sent as an exhibitioner from Threshfield.

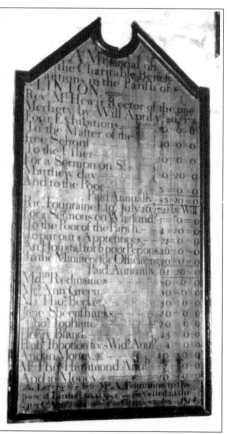

Fig. 24. Memorial Board, Linton Church

The first two names from the earlier Threshfield list are John Inman, 1684, and Goodgionis Jackman, 1686. The date given is when each went up to Cambridge.

Corresponding entries on the Cambridge list are:

'John Inman, admitted sizar, aged 18 at St. John's, May 23, 1684, son of Robert, husbandman, deceased, born at Woodhouse, Yorkshire, school Threshfield (Mr. Motley), matriculated 1685, BA 1687- 8'

'Goodgionis Jackman, admitted pensioner at St. John's, May 12, 1686, son of John, gentleman of Skipton, Yorkshire, baptized there 1668-9, school Threshfield (Mr. Motley), matriculated 1686, admitted at the Middle Temple, June 24, 1687, called to the Bar, May 18, 1694.' [3]

There were also one or two odd discrepancies. Robert Hodgson who went up to Cambridge in 1711 was said in the Threshfield lists to be the son of a farrier, but in the Cambridge lists to be the son of a furrier.

George Proctor, 1716, whose father was said to be a carrier in the Threshfield list, was in the Cambridge lists as a currier, again with a 'u'.

Which of them was right? If they made a mistake, how did the mistake occur? Perhaps whoever wrote the original list used an open-topped 'a' which was, in Cambridge, mistaken for a 'u'.

The Threshfield lists showed 48 exhibitioners. The Cambridge list gave their status while at Cambridge: there was one 'pensioner' and all the rest were 'sizars'. A pensioner at Cambridge University was an undergraduate who paid for his own commons, or rations: a person who paid his own way, or his parents did. A sizar was an undergraduate who received an allowance from the college enabling him to study. The name indicated that the person so admitted received free 'sizes', that is to say, 'free allowances or portions of bread and drink'. Formerly the sizars also performed the duties now discharged by college servants. In our case, of course, the sizars were paid by Matthew Hewitt's benefaction. The proportion of sizars among the Threshfield exhibitioners was larger than among Cambridge undergraduates in general, which suggested that Matthew Hewitt accomplished his aim of enabling people to go to Cambridge who otherwise would not have been able to afford it.

The Threshfield lists gave the occupations of all but six of the fathers of the exhibitioners: twenty Husbandmen, four Gentleman, four Clerks, four Yeomen, a Hosier , a Carrier, a Farrier, an Institutor, a Maltster, a Tax-collector, a Tax gatherer; one Plumber, one Steward, one Freeholder, one 'Plebii', one Wool spinner, one Publican. An institutor was probably an instructor, and plebii perhaps commoners? 26 exhibitioners were from Wharfedale, 3 from Wensleydale, 2 from York. The most distant places they came from were Acaster near Selby, Balderstones near Preston, and Halifax.

What happened to those men after leaving Threshfield for St Johns? Two died as undergraduates and are buried in Cambridge. Two became lawyers, and two schoolmasters (one at Ermysted's, Skipton). Twentyseven took Holy Orders, and held livings in Yorkshire (13), Norfolk (3), and one each in Derbyshire, Lancashire, Northumberland, Nottinghamshire and one (possibly) in Jamaica. The Cambridge list noted a *'Joseph Stoney of Trelawney, Jamaica, who died July 1719'* [5] and named another Joseph Stoney who went up in 1746. So most of the boys' fathers were husbandmen, and more than half of their sons became Anglican clergymen.

In other words, we could regard Threshfield School as part of a process by which sons of husbandmen were turned into Anglican clergy. A husbandman is one who cultivates the land, a farmer, but how far does it extend in either direction, upper or lower? It probably does not take in farm labourers, who were at that time illiterate; it does include people who we would think of as gentlemen farmers. There are two instances:

James Allen, of Gayle in Wensleydale, is said to be the son of a husbandman; the Allens of Gayle always maintained that they were gentlemen farmers, as were the family of William Sheepshanks, of Linton. They weren't necessarily poor people. James Allen of Gayle was an interesting character. The Cambridge list noted two James Allens of Gayle. One, who was the son of Leonard, husbandman, went up in 1710, and the other, son of Oswald, husbandman, went in 1731. During his time at Cambridge this second James went to Oxford and met Wesley, by whom he was influenced. He became first a Methodist, but then joined the Sandemanian sect. He left college after a year and went back to Gayle, where he founded and built the Sandemanian chapel and ministered there until his death on October 31, 1804. You may still go to Gayle and see what was the Sandemanian Chapel. It is now a Village Institute and has a little graveyard with the graves of various Allens in it. The most famous Sandemanian of all was the scientific genius, Michael Faraday.

We know a good deal about William Sheepshanks. He lived at the Metcalfe's farm in Linton, which is now called 'The Grange', though I understand it used to be called 'Sheepshanks'. Whitaker writes:

'William Sheepshanks was born in the village of Linton on the 8th March, 1740 of respected parents… His father, who, having no trade or profession, lived upon and farmed his own estate… He was a very sensible and intelligent man, so far superior to those among whom he lived and so disinterested in the application of his talents, that he was highly popular in his native village…His mother was a woman of very superior understanding.

He was educated at the grammar school of the parish and in 1761 was admitted to St. John's College, Cambridge… In vigour and clearness of understanding Mr. Sheepshanks was excelled by few… His spirits were lively and his conversation inexhaustibly fertile in anecdote and reflection…. His knowledge of common life in all its modes was that of an original and acute observer; his eyes were the most penetrating and expressive I ever beheld….His conversation had much…. originality and humour… When he could be prevailed upon to write at all, he wrote with clearness and force... But a constitutional indolence robbed him of the fame which he might have attained... His want of ambition was at least equal to his hatred of exertion.' [6]

The Minute and Account Book of the Governors and Feoffees of Burnsall School contains the following entry:

'December 21 1776. Memorandum that Mr. William Sheepshanks, Master of Arts, late fellow of St. John's College, Cambridge was then elected and also admitted schoolmaster of Burnsall' [Fn1]

Did he ever really teach at Burnsall? I have a suspicion that he really remained in Grassington and left all the teaching at Burnsall to a miserably paid £10 a year Usher.

Another person of interest was Simon Rudd, son of Simon, husbandman of Cubeck, Wensleydale He was admitted to St. John's in 1700, and became the Vicar of Aysgarth. The Rudd family is still prominent in that part of Wensleydale.

There was also a family called Mitton. John Mitton, son of Roger, a clerk, was born in Cambridge, went to school in Threshfield and was admitted to Cambridge University in 1705. Roger Mitton, who was presumably John's father, BA 1685-6, became Vicar of Kildwick, 1698-1705, and the Vicar of Skipton 1705-1740, was Rural Dean in 1723 and died in June 1740. The Cambridge list also noted another Roger Mitton, admitted in 1680, the son of Robert, a blacksmith of Starbotton, Kettlewell, Yorkshire, but there was no mention of his school.

Jeremy Fawkes, admitted to Cambridge in 1704, was born at Farnley, Yorkshire, the son of Nicholas, husbandman. He became Rector of Warmsworth, Yorkshire, 1716-1744. I thought that Jeremy Fawkes might, having been born at Farnley, be a relative of Guy Fawkes. This I think is still possible, although I haven't evidence for it, but to my great surprise, Guy Fawkes himself did appear in the Cambridge list.

The very last Threshfield exhibitioner of all, Gildard Jackson, went up to Cambridge in 1856. Gildard was born in Sculcoates, Yorkshire and became MA, Deacon, Priest, and Curate of Berwick-on-Tweed 1862-5; Rector of St. James the Less, Edinburgh 1865-98; Canon of St. Mary's Cathedral, Edinburgh; Honorary Canon of Edinburgh 1899-1915. He died at Guilford in Surrey in 1925.

The next question is, were there any really distinguished characters among these Threshfield scholars? John Tennant, born at Chapel House, Kilnsey, went up in 1739, and then proceeded to the Middle Temple where he became a Bencher (someone who holds a high position in the Inns of Court). He was also a Lent Reader for one year, which means he was a fairly distinguished lawyer. He is said to have been buried at Conistone though his name is not included in the Tennant memorial there.

Fn1 A Feoffee is a trustee invested with a freehold estate to hold in possession for a charitable purpose. OED

It might be interesting to have a hunt to see if one could find a John Tennant headstone in the graveyard, but any inscription from as long ago as that would now be more or less indecipherable.

How can we assess the achievements of Matthew Hewitt? Was it a good thing to turn the sons of husbandmen into Anglican clergy?

Well, surely they led more varied and interesting lives than they would have done had they remained on their fathers' farms. Most of these boys who went from Threshfield to St. John's, and then scattered themselves over the country as Anglican clergy, were good, honest, decent clergyman who did their jobs. But the very favourite character of them all is, for me, James Allen, who rejected the prevailing Anglicanism and went firmly back to Gayle and did his own thing.

Abstract from a talk given to the Local History Group 1990.

Sources:

1. Crowther, John (1930) Silva Gars. Keighley: Wadsworth and Co. The Royal Press.
2. Whitaker, Thomas (1878) third edition. History and Antiquities of the Deanery of Craven.
3. Venn, Michael Alumini Cantarbrigiensis, based on Admissions to St John's College 1630-1767. Material collected by Professor I.E. Mayor (1825-1916), a member of St John's College, Cambridge and Professor of Latin, and R.E. Cott, Master of St John's College, Cambridge The University Library, Cambridge.
4. Whitaker, 1878.

9. A Glimpse into the Classroom 1841-1904
Jean M. Booth

According to the 1841 census there was only one student in Grassington, aged 15. It is likely that he had private tuition. Most children were at work in the lead mines, in textiles or in domestic service by the age of eleven. In fact one or two eight year olds were in employment. There was a schoolmaster, John Harker, where was his school? Who were his pupils? In 1851 he is listed as schoolmaster and registrar and he may have been the first master of Grassington school, which opened in 1846. His name comes up there and also at Threshfield.

Also in 1851 the census records a schoolmistress, Louisa May Groom and a pupil teacher, Ellen Harker, possibly John's niece. By 1851, the school, now housing, which stands on Wood Lane near the junction with Station Road, was open. Miss

Ellen Eliza Lambert of Settle, a descendant of the Pearts who built Church House, gave land in trust for a school *"for persons of and in the township of Grassington"* and "adjoining hamlets". It was to be run according to the principles of the Established Church of England.

There were three rooms for a master or mistress or married couple to live in. There is a record of the rather sparse furnishings provided for the teacher in 1857; in 1867 Miss Coulson was provided with furniture, linen, china, floor coverings and household utensils. But who lived in the schoolhouse? At various times in the 1860s Inspectors asked why it was not occupied by staff. In 1845 Miss Rogers was to have £45 per year plus half the government grant. There is no record of when this sum was raised; in 1871 an Inspector commented that better pay would attract a better quality of staff.

The 1851 census described most children as "scholars". Some, in Grassington are listed as "at home", usually, but not always, children under school age. Scholars could be aged two! In one family a ten year old is a scholar, her eight year old sister an errand girl.

So in 1851 did John Harker, Miss Groom and Ellen Harker between them cope with 155 scholars? It is possible that this number was on roll but it would be rare for anything like that number to be present at the same time, judging by the evidence in the school log book. The average number on roll was about 100, attendance could be as low as 35.

Unfortunately the earliest log book deals with the period 1863-1904, so information about the school from 1845-1863 is sparse. However, an introduction to the log book written in 1982 by Ronald Harker provides some information. Himself an ex-pupil (1914-1921), he was proud of his family's connection with the school. In 1863 his great-aunt Mary Ann Harker was headmistress, unfortunately she died in 1867. Another relative, William Harker became an Attendance Officer in 1871 and remained so for fifty years. An aunt, Ada, was a pupil teacher in 1871 and was head from 1885-1892; another aunt, Amadine, was a pupil teacher in 1908 and Ronald's grandfather, Mathias Henry Harker was a manager in 1922.

John Harker, of whom mention has been made earlier, darts in and out of the school story. In 1865 Mary Ann Harker, who was ill, wrote "father is assisting me a little". He was in school but also tutoring pupil teachers at home. In1884 he was in school for a month or two when Mrs. Etherington died in November.

In its early days the school had many problems. It must be remembered that elementary education for all was not the norm until the passing of Forster's Act in 1870. Education became compulsory in 1881 when enough schools had been built. It was not free until 1891. From 1839 the government did give grants to elementary schools. These grants were dependent upon children reaching the required standard for their age group.

Government Inspectors visited annually, a fraught day for staff and pupils alike. So in earlier days staff were pioneers trying to persuade parents and pupils that education was worthwhile. Also some pupils were half timers working at Low Mill.

As the following list shows there were many changes of staff, stability came only after the arrival of Mr. and Mrs. Chapman in 1894.

1845	John Harker
1851	Louisa Maria Groom
1850's?	Miss Hall
1857	Miss Atkinson
1863	Mary Ann Harker. Died 1867
1867	Miss Coulson
1868	Mrs Spicer
1875	Ann Shepherd. Left in June
	Miss Elizabeth Gibson
1877	Miss E. E. Cockburn. Died June
1883	From August Mrs. Etherington, died November
	John Harker temporarily
1885	Mr. W. Townsend temporarily
1886	Ada Jane Harker
1892	Jessie May Norton. Resigned in June
1893	Miss Jennet Dean
	Miss Annie Dawson
1894	Mr. James Allan Chapman and
	Mrs. Jane Chapman

The changes and the illness of some teachers must have been difficult for pupils and pupil teachers. Small wonder that there were comments that their lessons were sometimes ill prepared and ineffective. The school did not always reach the standards required by the Inspectors and this occasionally meant that the full grant was unavailable. The Inspectors were supportive of staff efforts, well aware that they were struggling against absenteeism, unpunctuality and parent apathy or hostility.

In 1868 the Inspector felt that the school managers were not pressing for regular attendance and that parents wanted to dictate the curriculum. At this time boys over the age of eight were not admitted and it was thought that some parents wanted their girls to be proficient in fancy work and knitting rather than the 3r's.

There are frequent references in the log book to "unruly behaviour", e.g. in 1875 a boy was excluded because he "rebelled and used bad language".

Earlier in 1863 school opened with 50 "unruly pupils". Sometimes parents kept children at home if they had been chided for bad work or behaviour. There were complaints that children were overworked. In September 1882 one parent suggested his child should only do two sums in the day.

Mrs. Etherington introduced good conduct marks in 1883 and in 1894 Mr. Chapman introduced attendance tickets. Children were absent for many reasons, sometimes they were at home because parents could not or would not pay the school pence. In fact, when the weekly fee became 2d, some parents, including "farmers and business men", withdrew their children for a time. They were absent because they were helping with haymaking or cleaning the house for Christmas, Easter or Grassington Feast. In 1882 boys were "getting rushes from the moor".

Bad weather, as in the bad winters of 1875 and 1881 caused absences and lateness. In 1881 boys were late because "they could not water their cows".

Childhood illnesses are recorded, some which became less prevalent or dangerous because of immunisation. Measles is mentioned in 1868 and 1893. Also in 1893 there was smallpox, whooping cough and mumps. In 1863 one child died of croup; in 1866 three died of diphtheria.

Some absences were because of interesting local events, Kilnsey Show, Skipton Fair, Arncliffe Flower Show, the annual otter hunt. In 1875 children stayed away to watch the cavalry go by.

There were approved absences: for a church service in1866 when "cattle plague" was raging, for the opening of the Devonshire Institute in 1878 and for the opening of Hebden Church in 1884. There was a week's holiday granted in 1897 for Queen Victoria's Diamond Jubilee and in 1900 a half holiday was given when Ladysmith was relieved. In 1900 the scholars were complimented on the part they played by being in the procession when the first sod was cut for the Grassington Railway.

By that time the curriculum had widened, music, nature study being introduced and it is good to record the appearance of swings in the playground in 1893.

A hundred years on Grassington School still continues, albeit in a different building, where a dedicated staff helps the present generation to meet the challenges of the twenty first century.

Sources:

A. Primary

a. The 1841 and 1851 census returns

b. Grassington School Log Book 1863-1904

c. Trust Deed of the first Grassington Primary School.

B. Secondary

a. Ancestral Trails. Mark Herber

b. Approaches to Local History. Alan Rogers.

Acknowledgements

1. Peter Fethney for producing census returns in typescript.

2. Helen Clayton, The Headmistress of Grassington School, for granting access to the school Log Book.

The First Grassington Primary School: The 1845 Trust Deed
Bill Rhodes

In the first part of the nineteenth century few children were taught to read or write. Most people were poor in those days, and only those parents who were wealthy enough could send their children to school or employ a teacher to teach them in their own homes. From about 1842 the Church of England began setting up schools such as the one in Grassington so that more children could be educated. Even then, children had to bring a few pence each week to pay for their education.

In 1870 the Government also founded schools, and later still changed the law so that all children had to go to school, whether they liked it or not.

In the early 1990s the governors of Grassington Church of England Primary School searched for the original trust deed of the school from the date of its opening in 1845. It was finally located in the archives of Bradford Cathedral, where it remains. A copy was handed to the Field Society and is reproduced below.

The deed was written in 1845 when the school was built and is an agreement under which Ellen Eliza Lambert gave the land for the purposes of building a school. It also makes some rules about how the school was to be run. It says 'for ever' but laws have changed since then and few of these rules are now followed.

It is very hard to read, as it has faded. The legal wording seems rather formal; for instance, a piece of land is called a 'parcel of land'.

The school was relocated to larger, modern premises in 1976, and the original building on Wood Lane was converted into five cottages.

The school still has strong associations with the parish of Linton-in-Craven and the Rector remains chairman of governors. However, he no longer has the sole power to appoint staff, and the head teacher is no longer obliged to live on the premises.

THE TRUST DEED

I, Ellen Eliza Lambert of Settle in the County of York, Spinster, under the authority of an Act passed in the fifth year of the reign of Her Majesty Queen Victoria, instituted an Act for affording further facilities for the Conveyance and Endowment of sites for Schools DO hereby freely and voluntarily, and without any valuable consideration, grant and convey to The Reverend Henry Crofts, a clerk, Rector of the first mediety of the parish of Linton in the West Riding of the County of York and to Joseph Mason of Grassington in the said parish, Thomas Atkinson of Linton in the same parish, Farmer, Richard Walker of Hebden Bank Top in the same parish, Farmer, and John Calvert of Threshfield, Innkeeper, the Church wardens of the said parish, and to their respective successors for ever ALL THAT parcel of Land situate at Grassington in the parish of Linton aforesaid, heretofore part of a close of Land there called the Croft, otherwise Townend Croft in the occupation of William Wall a Tenant to the said Ellen Eliza Lambert but now walled, fenced or staked off and separated there from which said parcel of Land intended to be hereby conveyed contains one rood and seventeen perches, or thereabouts in statute measure, be the same more or less, and is bounded on the east by the back lane or road leading from Grassington aforesaid to Conistone, on the west by the said close of Land, called the Croft, otherwise Townend Croft, on the North by land belonging to Messieurs Husband and Mann, and on the south by other land belonging to me called Crow Trees Garth; Together with all ways, watercourses, rights, privileges and appurtenances whatsoever, to the said parcel of Land above described in any ways appertaining; And all my right title and interest to and in the same, as purchaser thereof in fee simple from the Reverend William Peart of Hulse Wood near Bexley in the County of Kent, Clerk: TO HOLD unto and to the use of the said Henry Crofts, Joseph Mason, Thomas Atkinson, Richard Walker and John Calvert and their respective successors, as such Rector and Churchwardens as aforesaid henceforth in perpetual succession for the purposes of the said clerk, and to be applied as a site for a School or Schools for poor persons of and in the Township of Grassington aforesaid and for such other poor persons of and in any other Township or Hamlet adjoining or near thereto as the said Henry Crofts and his successors in the said Rectory shall, from time to time, think proper to admit and receive and for the residence of the Teacher or Teachers of such School or Schools, and for no other purpose whatsoever: such School or Schools to be always in union with "The National Society for promoting the Education of the poor in the principles of the Established Church", and conducted according to its principles, and for the furtherance of its ends and designs; and to be under the sole management and control of the said Henry Crofts and his successors, Rectors of the First Mediety of the Parish of Linton aforesaid; by whom the Master and Mistress shall, from time to time, be appointed and dismissed; and to be open at all reasonable times; to the Inspector or Inspectors for the time being appointed or to be appointed as conformably to the Order in Council dated the fourth day of August one thousand eight hundred and forty. PROVIDED that if at any time the Rector of the First Mediety of the said Parish of Linton for the time being should be incapable or unwilling to act in the management and control of the said School, or should not be resident in the said Parish or within five miles of the same, then the said School shall be under the management and control of the Officiating Minister, for the time being, of the said First Mediety of the said Parish, and if at any time neither such Rector nor such Officiating Minister shall be willing to undertake the management and control of the said School, then the Bishop of the Diocese, within which the said Parish shall be situated, shall select a Committee of persons (not exceeding five) resident in the said Parish, or within five miles of it, to whom the managements and control of the said School shall be entrusted, until the Rector or Officiating Minister shall have given notice in writing, to the said Bishop, of his willingness to undertake the same, and the said Ellen Eliza Lambert shall be satisfied therewith. IN WITNESS thereof the conveying and other parties have hereunto set their hands and seals, the twenty eighth day of March in the year of our Lord one thousand eight hundred and forty five.

Ellen Eliza Lambert Thomas Atkinson

Henry Crofts Richard Walker

Joseph Mason John Calvert

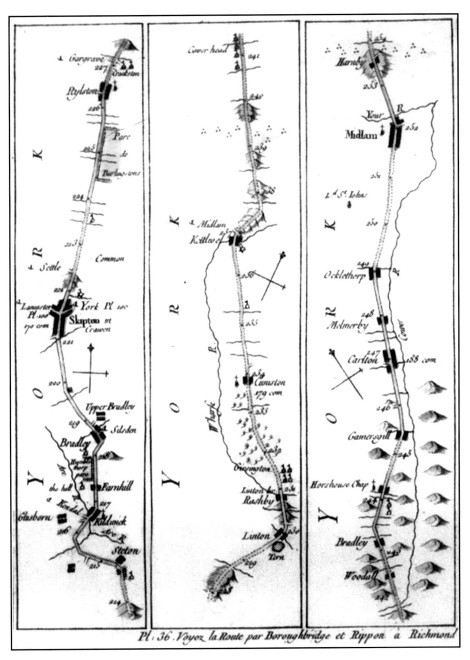

Map by John Senex, Edition 1719-1750.
Plate 36

Low Mill Lane (Courtesy of Christopher Payne)

Barden Tower (Courtesy of R White. YDNP)

Kilnsey (Photo Jane Hargreaves)

The Village of Conistone (Photo Phyllida Oates)

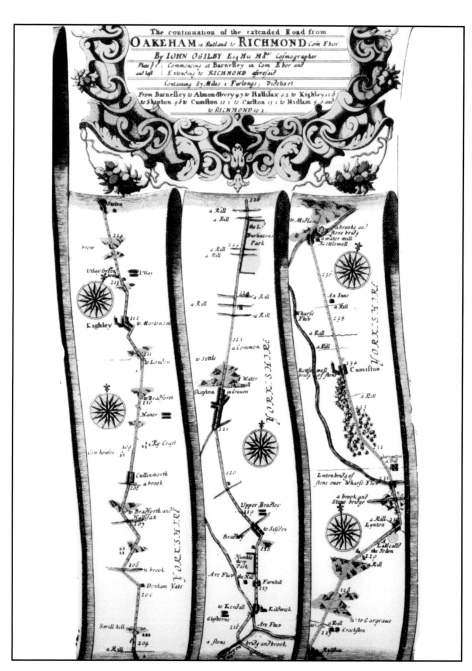

Britannia Vol. 1 John Ogilby Plate 49

MDCLXXV 1765

Religious Non-Conformity

10. Friends In Truth: The Quakers of Upper Wharfedale

Richard Harland

In May 1652 the 28 year-old George Fox from Leicestershire was travelling through West Yorkshire, brimming over with a commitment to spread his belief that in each one of us there lies a seed of the Spirit that grows through nurturing when we open it to God's guidance.

This 'Truth', as he described it, lay within the Christian faith, yet was independent of sacraments, ritual or priests, nurtured instead by meeting with like-minded folk in meetings for worship based on simplicity, silence instead of spoken ritual, and 'a priesthood of all believers.'

It was a clear day, and from Pendle Hill he saw the fells of the western dales and the glistening of Morecambe Bay with the Lakeland foothills beyond. Something told him he would find receptive hearers there.

And so it proved, most strikingly, among both the congregations of the established church and the network of dissenters who called themselves 'Seekers.' Arriving in Langstrothdale at the head of Wharfedale, he asked to spend the night at Scarhouse, above Hubberholme (Fig. 25), where he was welcomed by Cicely Tennant, her son James and his wife Elizabeth, and their nine-year-old son, young James. By the next morning those in the little household were beginning to discover the experience of which he spoke. Here is his own account of these few hours, remembered and dictated a quarter of a century later:

'So I came through the dales to a man's house, one Tennant, and I was moved to speak to the family, and as I was turning away from them I was moved to turn again and declare God's everlasting Truth to him and he was convinced, and his family, and lived and died in the Truth.'

The Tennants spread the message and formed a local network. Within months this was replicated through much of the land. These folk called themselves 'Friends in Truth' or simply 'Friends'. Others called them 'Quakers,' a nickname for various dissidents, and for Friends, it stuck. Their successors today are happy with either name, Friends or Quakers.

The building blocks of the Scarhouse network were made up by little groups of Friends. Those living in Littondale, some as far away as Penyghent, met at Arncliffe or Hawkswick; in Langstrothdale they met at Deepdale, Scarhouse and Cray, and in Upper Wharfedale at Buckden and Starbotton. Others met in Upper Bishopdale.

None of these groups left any records, but we get glimpses, as in a letter of 1654 from a Sedbergh Friend, for example:

'I came the last weeke, and had one meeting in Littondale where are some few friends come out and others coming out, and people pretty moderate and willing to heare, praised be the Lord, and soe amongst them my spirit was refreshed.'

To live by this faith took pluck and sacrifice. For the 36 years of the Commonwealth and from 1660 under the Stuarts, religious tolerance fluctuated. In 1655 James

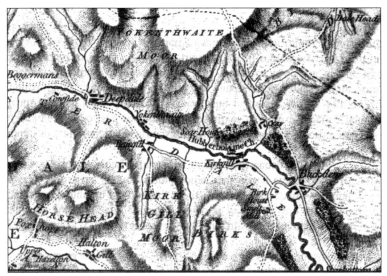

Fig. 25. Hubberholme and Deepdale: from Thomas Jeffreys The County of York Survey'd. 1775 – The Environs of Sedbergh, Dent, Hawes and Settle.

Tennant was gaoled in York Castle for not paying tithes to support the established church he had left and for the greater crime of refusing to swear to the truth of his statements on oath in Court; to do that would mean accepting a double standard, and truth in all his dealings was basic to his Quaker faith. The putrid gaol destroyed his health and led to his early death.

From 1662 it was a crime even to meet for silent worship, and several in the Scarhouse network went to gaol for this. For pastoral and other church affairs, those who were able gathered at Scarhouse each month.

Littondale Friends could be there and back in a day, most others lived within an hour's walk, and for the cluster at Raisgill, Yockenthwaite, Deepdale, New House and Cowside House it would seem no distance. They upheld one another in their faith and in Quakerly everyday conduct; they collected for the dependents of Friends in gaol, and in 1666 they sent money for victims of London's great fire.

Every month they looked for two or more members to attend the area meeting, held at Skipton in the mid 1660s and at Settle from 1669, there to continue for almost the next two centuries. They joined Friends from Airton, Bentham, Bowland, Rylstone, Selside and Settle. Most months two or more, especially those with horses, were ready to make the 24 mile return journey. Among them went young James Tennant and his wife. In this way the stay-at-homes were fed with news. Whether on foot or horseback, the tracks over the fells were a delight in fine weather but risky in the dark months when the weather could turn bad.

Fig. 26. Drawing of The 1698 Datestone at Scar House. National Trust. drawing by Dan Powell

In 1674, upon the death of another James Tennant, the family procured a smooth stone and incised upon it 'IT 1674' (at that time J was carved as I), and no doubt placed it in the burial ground beside the house. However by the early 1700s Friends had come to regard gravestones as inconsistent with living simply, and also, because of their cost, as a discrimination against the poor. No more were erected in Scarhouse burial ground, and in 1717 it was advised that existing ones be removed, so the burial ground has no stones. That would be when James Tennant's stone became a butter-shelf in the larder, where it can still be seen.

In April 1677, twenty-five years after his first visit, George Fox, with a few companions, came again to Scarhouse, on their way from Ulverston to London. Riding over the tops from Countersett, by Semerwater in Wensleydale, deep snow made their journey a struggle, and he was in frail health, yet upon arrival he spoke for several hours with those who had gathered. The occasion had been notified as a 'general meeting', and some had come from as far as Sedbergh, Skipton and Bentham. Elizabeth Tennant, the first James Tennant's widow, who knew him from 1652, rejoiced to see him. Her son James, and his wife Ann, who had followed both with the farm and in the faith, must have felt proud to entertain George Fox.

Scarhouse general meetings of Friends from far and wide became a tradition, and on each occasion true Dales hospitality would be enjoyed.

In 1698 James and Ann remodelled the house; a stone over the door gives their initials 'IAT 1698' (Fig. 26). Further modernisation in 1876 meant removing a third storey garret, rebuilding the front wall, and replacing the stone staircase in wood. The main rooms remained unchanged.

Friends met in the left-hand upstairs chamber, as seen facing the building, and also in the right-hand downstairs parlour. An inventory made at James' death in 1719 vividly revealed how those rooms were laid out for Friends' meetings. In the upstairs room were a dozen chairs, a round table and a chest of drawers; nothing else. In the bedroom across the landing were another half dozen chairs ready to carry in. The downstairs room had just six chairs and a square table. Both rooms have now been made a little smaller by partitioning.

Scarhouse burial ground is marked by towering sycamores; it lies a stone's throw from the house, beyond the ancient orchard. In 1709 James Tennant had put it in trust to be used for an outside meeting place as well as for burial; one can picture a crowded meeting here for worship when the house was too small. Fourteen burials were recorded between 1680 and 1800 and there may have been others. The place still evokes tender thoughts.

After James Tennant's death the house passed out of Quaker hands, so the rooms were no longer available to Friends. Instead they met on alternate weeks at Starbotton and Deepdale, and at Arncliffe and Hawkswick, and changed the name of this faith-community from Scarhouse Meeting to Langstroth Meeting. This carried on with strength and energy for more than two further generations, but eventually numbers dropped; Friends moved away to marry or to join relatives, and for less harsh livelihoods. This Meeting came to an end in 1802, just 150 years after George Fox's ground-breaking visit. The role of Scarhouse had been crucial for Friends in Langstrothdale during the first 67 years of the establishment of the Quaker movement in this area.

Eventually the historic house and burial ground at Scarhouse were acquired by Graham and David Watson, who in 1989 included them with much other Wharfedale property in a munificent gift to the National Trust. The old orchard has now been replanted with fruit trees and the burial ground is tended, while the house with its stunning views is let for self-catering holidays, its tasteful furnishing taking account of Quaker simplicity.

Sources

See Appendix C

11. Witness to the Faith of Religious Independence The Congregationalists

Brontë Bedford-Payne

Before the time of Oliver Cromwell there were, broadly speaking, two denominations of practising Christians in England, the Roman Catholics and from the reign of Henry VIII, the emergent Church of England, whose followers were known as Protestants. During the Commonwealth, dissenters began to emerge, forming independent groups of believers who worked as equals in the ordering of religious meetings known as conventicles. [Fn1]

Fig. 27. Grassington Congregational Chapel built in 1811

The religious revival of the 17th and 18th centuries produced several movements: Presbyterians, Wesleyan Methodists, Baptists, Quakers, and Independents, as the early Congregationalists were called.

Fn1 A conventicle was a secret or unlawful religious meeting, usually of nonconformists.

66

Independents were one of the groups who flourished in the 1640-1660 period, during the Civil War and the Commonwealth, but between then and the passing of the Act of Toleration in 1689 during the reign of James II, persecution of non-Anglicans by the restored monarchy caused their numbers to dwindle.

The Congregationalists were the earliest distinct group of dissenters known in the Yorkshire Dales.

The district around Winterburn was, in the mid 17th century, a possession of General Lambert of Calton Hall. This was the same Lambert who had commanded Cromwell's army in Yorkshire at the time of the siege of Skipton Castle and who officiated as Lord Chamberlain at the investiture of Cromwell in 1653. His daughter-in-law, Barbara Lambert, *'who seems to have inherited the spirit and sacrificial zeal of the Puritans, took the whole of the Craven area under her peculiar spiritual care'* at a time when the restoration of the Monarchy in 1660 meant the expulsion of many nonconformist preachers. Some men found both asylum and a place to preach in the open air in the Yorkshire Dales.

Oliver Heywood, one of the founding fathers of the congregational movement and instrumental in the building not only of the chapel at Winterburn but also the one at Horton-in-Craven, reveals in his diary how the influence of Mistress Barbara, as she was affectionately known, ensured that, to him, the doors of Calton Hall were ever open, and gave him access to the farmhouses, where *'I had the opportunity and the security of the place.'*

In 1694 in Winterburn, the house of Thomas Whalley was certified as a Meeting House for Protestant Dissenters. In 1703 Whalley bought two cottages and a parcel of land on which he funded the building of a 'House for God' completed in 1704.

The foundation deed is an indenture dated 7th November 1704 and *'conveys to the trustees a newly erected chapel, oratory and meeting place ... to be used as a meeting place etc. and assembly of a particular church or congregation of PROTESTANTS dissenting from the Church of England for the free exercise of their Divine and Religious Worship therein ...'* On 13th October 1708, Barbara Lambert left the sum of £100 for the support of its minister.

Early Grassington Congregationalists sometimes walked the 6 miles to Winterburn Chapel, but more frequently found spiritual nourishment in cottage meetings or services held by the river. These meetings were led by independent laymen from other chapels or by students from the Airedale Academy at Idle near Bradford. (Every Sunday, from their second year of study onwards, these young men were sent out to preach all over the area.) Amos Blackburn, who entered the college in 1818 aged 17 years, wrote *'It is three months since I commenced preaching the Gospel, in which time I have preached between 40 and 50 times, and have walked 500 miles for that purpose.'*

When, in 1811, the congregation in Grassington became too large to be accommodated in cottages, a subscription list for the first chapel was drawn up and building started immediately – building first, parson second. Such was the enthusiasm that the new chapel (Fig. 27) was quickly completed, though a debt of £250 took 50 years to pay back.

The first service was held on Christmas Day that same year. In 1812, the Rev. John Calvert, one of the students at the Idle Academy, accepted the position of Minister and was ordained in 1813. His immediate duty was to draw up a covenant and determine who should sign it. This Covenant, now framed, hangs on a wall in the chapel. It was signed by Robert Somerville and William Simpson, their wives, and others, whose names are still familiar in the village: Wilson, Lee, Pattinson, Verity, Summergill, and Harker. William Simpson was elected Deacon, and remained the only one for 21 years.

The Covenant itself makes impressive reading:

'We, who were by nature sinners ready to perish, having by the good Spirit and abundant grace of God been led to see our dreadful state by nature, as fallen in Adam, and far from God; and having, we trust, tasted of the Grace of God in converting, promised, and communicated Mercy; we do sincerely, unfeignedly and without reserve, desire to give up ourselves to the Lord, and to each other; to walk together in all the Commandments and Ordinances of the Lord, blameless: to watch over one another in love; to exhort with diligence; rebuke with meekness and without partiality; and to pray for and seek the edification of each other in all things pertaining to Life and Godliness.

We profess ourselves to be of that persuasion which is generally called Calvinistic, though we call no man Lord or Master in what we profess, but receive the whole Word of God, as the rule of our faith, and the test of our experience. The Assembly's Catechism comes the nearest to our sentiments of any published opinions, as having a tendency to humble the sinner, exalt the Saviour, and promote holiness in heart and life.

With respect to our Church government, we call ourselves Independents or Congregationalists, readily receiving the advice of any other similar Society if we see that we need the same, but not to be under the jurisdiction of any other person or society whatever.'

From 1830 the fortunes of the chapel began to decline, reflecting the fluctuating fortunes of the local textile and lead mining industries in which most of the congregation were employed. Linton Mill closed in the 1840s and in 1856 the Birkbecks sold both Scawgill and Grassington Low Mill, while later in the century lead mining in the area drew to a close. Although census returns for Grassington indicate that the population numbers were high, the cottages in the terraces along Garrs Lane and Chapel Street housing very large families, the actual working population in the village dropped.

Chapel records show that during this time there were a large number of young people buried in the churchyard, leaving only a handful of middle-aged and elderly folk to carry on the good work at the chapel. These early deaths may well have been a result of poor working conditions in the mills and in the mines, coupled with overcrowding and poor sanitation in the houses. Nationally, life expectancy during the nineteenth century was low; poverty and hardship were the norm.

By 1852 the last minister at the Congregational Chapel had left and the congregation were in a pitiable state, with the debt of £250 unredeemed. For the next 35 years the pulpit was supplied by students from Airedale Academy, and ministers from other chapels. Despite the difficulties, the chapel was re-roofed in 1861, in celebration of the church's golden jubilee. Using voluntary labour the work was completed at a cost of £100, raised without incurring any new debts, although the chapel was still burdened by the original one. Two local benefactors, Alderman James Law and Benjamin Harrison then promised £100 each to help clear this, on condition that the remainder could be raised locally. The appeal was successful, and not only was the debt cleared, but a nearby cottage was bought for use as a classroom, and in the church, most of the old box pews, now seen only in the gallery, were replaced.

By 1869 Reverend Bailey Harker, in his book Rambles in Upper Wharfedale, was able to comment. *'In connection with the Chapel is a burial ground, several cottages, a large garden and a parsonage; it is the only Chapel in the town which is clear of debt.'* Born in Garrs Hill in 1843, Bailey Harker became an influential member of the Grassington community after 1907, when he retired and returned to his home village.

He had been a Minister of the Congregational Church since 1867 and in Grassington he was frequently called to act as pastor. Harker was a fellow of the Royal Horticultural Society, and he not only founded the Wharfedale Antiquarian Exploration Society but also found time to campaign long and tirelessly for the building of the Skipton to Grassington railway.

From 1908 Grassington Chapel prospered again, and *'...a great quickening, spiritually and financially, was produced, when the Church at Skipton (St. Andrew's) volunteered pastoral oversight.'* From that time visiting preachers came regularly and the centenary was joyfully celebrated in 1911 when a pamphlet called Centenary History was produced.

In 1922, after 33 years without a pastor of its own, the Reverend Benjamin Albert Millard was appointed. Under his ministry, which lasted until 1929, church membership remained steady in number at 40 (with children outnumbering adults in 1929). Over £1,000 was raised to improve the church and the manse, including the installation of an organ and electricity.

In the late 20th century, a smaller manse was acquired and the original one became a private house. In the chapel the ceiling was lowered to shut off the balcony, and a new pulpit designed to allow the dais to be used for informal styles of worship.

Written evidence has revealed very little of the worshippers who crowded the chapel for services throughout the 19th century. The nearest we can get to those early generations of men and women, boys and girls is to imagine the foundation of their chapel, when, 'in the presence of witnesses from other churches, intending members stood in a circle, hand clasping hand, and solemnly pledged themselves to the Covenant which they then signed.'

Sources:

Robinson, Angela: Minister, Congregational Church 1978-1986: Unpublished notes

Morkill, John W (1933) The Parish of Kirkby Malhamdale, Gloucester: John Bellows

Spence, Richard T (1991) Skipton Castle in the Great Civil War 1642-1645, Otley: Smith Settle

Whitehead, Thomas (1930) History of the Dales Congregational Churches, Keighley: Feather Bros

On Long Ridge, Middleton Moor

12. Wesley's Vision: The Age of Chapel Building

Christine Bell

Wesleyan Methodism sprang from John Wesley's beliefs on how the religious life should be led and how personal salvation could be sought and found. From the 1730's John Wesley, his younger brother Charles, and their followers, preached throughout the kingdom in the open air or in barns, inspiring others in turn to follow them. Those moved by what they had heard organised themselves into small groups, meeting in members' homes.

The itinerant preachers who first held services and converted people in Upper Wharfedale were probably connected with William Grimshaw. Grimshaw, a curate at Haworth, was an early convert in the West Riding. His preaching circuit, known as the Great Haworth Round, covered a vast area from Birstall in the south to Whitehaven in the north, Pateley Bridge in the east and Preston in the west. After his death in 1763, the centre of the circuit moved from Haworth.

Early records of the Haworth/Keighley circuit provide the key to our understanding of the early Methodists in Upper Wharfedale. The account book for 1763 shows that Methodists in Skyrethorns, amongst whom are listed a publican, a cordwainer (cobbler) and a spinner, paid dues of 7s. in January, April and October. In Grassington in 1776 there was one payment of 5s. 6d. Other early societies were set up in Hebden, Burnsall and Skyreholme, with numbers of members ranging from 14 to 22.

During these early years John Wesley preached outside Plett's Barn in Grassington on 1st May 1780 and on 29th April 1782; there is a commemorative plaque marking the place and occasion. From 1801, the villages of Upper Wharfedale are no longer mentioned in the Keighley records; it is assumed that they became part of a new circuit based on Skipton. In 1810, Grassington became the head of its own circuit, with an area of influence from Barden to Buckden, and possibly beyond into Littondale and Langstrothdale.

The 19th century was the age of chapel building. The first chapels to be built were at Grassington in 1811 and at Buckden and Hebden around the same date. Little is known about these. The last two were rebuilt in 1877 and 1892. The present chapel in Grassington was first used as a meeting-house in 1810 and opened as a chapel in 1811. It is not clear whether this chapel was newly built or was a conversion of a previous one. In 1825 the present facade, gallery and pews were added. The schoolroom was built and a cottage bought in 1879. Wesleyan chapels were built in Kettlewell in 1835, Burnsall 1840, Starbotton 1860, Coniston 1865, and Barden in 1884. Hetton and Cracoe chapels, part of the Skipton circuit, were built in 1859 and 1881.

It is clear from early Grassington circuit records that Methodist Societies were also established in places where there were no chapels, as at Skyreholme, Litton, Arncliffe, Thorpe, Yockenthwaite, Skyrethorns, Linton, Hawkswick and Threshfield. A preaching plan of 1843 lists 15 villages where services took place. Grassington and Kettlewell had 3 Sunday services, and 4 other villages each had two. By this time, Wesleyan chapels were not the only Methodist places of worship; Primitive Methodists or Ranters had also begun to spread their mission of revival into Upper Wharfedale, and several new chapels were built: Grassington, Hebden, Kettlewell, Threshfield and Howgill, now known as Barden Chapel.

During the 19th century 8 Wesleyan and 5 Primitive Methodist chapels in all were built. In 1902 the old Burnsall chapel was rebuilt.

However after the First World War social habits altered and at the same time Wharfedale's labour-intensive occupations of farming, mining and textiles declined markedly. The chapels had been built at a time of religious revival, when the Sunday routine of 'going to chapel' was an outward show of religious conviction as well as a focus of social intercourse.

If one local family were Methodists, then their support was usually enough to build and maintain a particular chapel but many operated on a financial knife edge and perhaps only needed a single change in circumstances to fail.

Support for Methodism continued into the third decade of the 20th Century, but in 1926 Conistone Chapel closed. In 1932, the Methodist Union combined various strands of Methodism and caused many of the chapels to close, not only in Upper Wharfedale but throughout the country.

Now, at the beginning of the 21st Century, Grassington no longer has its own circuit but has joined with Skipton to become the Skipton and Grassington Circuit. Chapels at Grassington, Threshfield, Hebden and Burnsall continue to hold services. Although the age of chapel-building is unlikely to return, fortunately many of those 19th century chapels are still standing as a witness to the faith of those who built them.

Source

Haworth/Keighley circuit records, 1763

13. Chapel Folk
Primitive Methodists in Howgill and Skyreholme

Christine Bell

By 1836, when Howgill Primitive Methodist chapel (Fig. 26) was built, the Wesleyan Methodist tradition was well established throughout the land. Several other chapels had been built in Wharfedale and there were other places, too, where people met for prayer and worship. As often happens within religious organisations, some people found the status quo too restrictive, so in 1819 a group known as the Primitive Methodists or Ranters began to spread their zealous form of Christianity throughout the north of England. They were led by William Clowes, based in Hull, who travelled widely, being particularly welcomed in Silsden, where a circuit of chapels was formed. Members of this revival movement formed the Grassington Mission in 1834-5 and from this came the initiative to build Primitive Methodist chapels in Grassington, Hebden, Howgill and possibly Kettlewell.

For many years the chapel at Howgill was known as Barden Primitive Methodist Chapel. The men of Barden paid £10 to Thomas Inman, yeoman of Barden, with a holding of 54 acres in Howgill, for '...*a certain close of land called Lower Haugh Close in Appletreewick... upon special trust and the intent that a chapel or meeting house and school should be erected by the members of the said Primitive Methodist Connection at Barden'.* [1]

This particular piece of land is likely to have been the only plot available to such a radical band of dissenters, who might well have met considerable resistance from the 6th Duke of Devonshire had they proposed to establish a chapel on his adjacent estate in Barden.

The chapel was built on a site convenient for worshippers who would have come from all directions, converging on the bridge over Howgill Beck at Haugh Mill, on the road between Appletreewick and Barden Tower. Stepping stones and the wooden footbridge over the river Wharfe provided an important link with the hamlet of Drebley. However, it was not a very convenient site on which to erect a building, as Lower Haugh Close was a small plot wedged into the side of a very steep hill. The chapel is so close to the road it is difficult to imagine where ponies and traps could have been left during services. Within, the pulpit and choir are, placed unusually, on the immediate left of the door, and the pews rise steeply to the back of the building, perhaps because of this difficult terrain. [2]

It is likely that at the time of building the chapel was simply furnished.

The first trustees, listed below, borrowed £160 from William Clarkson of Silsden to build the chapel, and they were responsible for repaying the debt and the upkeep of the building:

Abraham Fortune of Silsden, nail maker

William Hebden of Addingham, draper

Thomas Holmes of Barden, farmer of 22 acres

John Inman of Skyreholme, farmer

Thomas Eastwood of Skyreholme, cotton spinner

John Willan of Grassington, cordwainer

John Whittaker of Grassington, miner

John Rodwell of Linton, miner

John Harrison of Linton, wool sorter

Henry Rodgers of Linton, woolcomber

Robert Birch of Linton, woolcomber

Thomas Howson of Hebden, weaver [3]

In the years that followed the building of the chapel, the zeal and fervour of the revival faded, support dwindled, and, in common with those of many such chapels, the Trustees were in debt for a long time.

Fig. 28. Howgill Primitive Methodist Chapel
(photo Heather Beaumont)

The debt remained unredeemed and in 1841 Howgill and Grassington chapels were offered to the Pateley Bridge circuit, but the offer was declined. However, the chapel did not close, and by 1863 new trustees had been appointed. Of those listed above, only five were still living and all these had moved elsewhere: William Hebden had moved to Calverly and was now a warp dresser, Thomas Eastwood had become a worsted spinner in East Marton, John Willan, still a cordwainer, had moved to Skipton, John Harrison, wool sorter, to East Marton and Thomas Howson, weaver, to Ingleton.

The new trustees elected in 1863 were as follows:

> Thomas Russell of Grassington, minister of the Gospel
>
> William Chapman, of Grassington, shoemaker
>
> Marmaduke Reynard of Skyreholme, farmer
>
> Thomas Inman of Skyreholme, labourer
>
> John Broadley of Skyreholme, lead miner
>
> John Turner of Hartlington, bobbin turner
>
> William Holmes, of Howgill, farmer
>
> John Birts of Grassington, lead miner [4]

Prominent among these was the minister, Thomas Russell, who had taken over the Grassington Mission in the early 1860s. A contemporary indenture shows that by now the original debt to William Clarkson had been paid off, but it is clear from the minister's writings that there were other debts. In 1865 he moved to a circuit in St Albans and, at the request of Hugh Bourne, one of the founders of Primitive Methodism, wrote his autobiography.

One chapter headed 'Among the Yorkshire Hills – Varied Experiences', refers to Howgill chapel and the difficulties he encountered:-

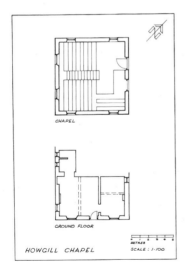

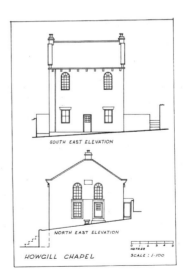

Fig. 29a & 29b. Plans of Howgill Chapel

'Directly almost on Grassington getting on its feet, Barden chapel money was called in. There was £260 on a small chapel, with a dwelling under it, and the foundations were saturated with springs, so that the house floor was often covered with water. I got some drainage tiles from Skipton, and our friends dug out to the back wall, where the water was pent up, and no way out for it. But we got a clear passage, and at the cost of nearly £20 made the whole tenantable. We got the debt down to £65, which two of our friends kindly lent on notes of hand; so that this long and hard struggle, which gave me a great deal of extra toil, sometimes with bleeding and blistered feet, was all settled, and the house was made a comfortable residence, and the chapel a respectable place, and some good was done'. [5]

Probably earlier than the end of the 1800s, there were strong links between the chapel and the Lumb family, who had already established paper-mills in the Skipton area. In 1874 a former corn mill in Skyreholme was purchased by William Whitely and his partner Thomas Lumb, who had been born in Barkisland, Halifax. They began to make pressed board, possibly from shoddy [Fn1] collected from the West Riding. Banquet House in Skyreholme became the Lumb's family home, named after the house in which Thomas was born. Lumb was a local preacher and often travelled in the Ministry as far as Horsehouse in Coverdale. He and his son Benjamin were both listed as trustees of Howgill Chapel on a document of 1896, and again on one dated 1931. One would not perhaps associate a well-to-do family with the beliefs of Primitive Methodism, but by the later 19th century the sect's more radical elements had declined; in any case Howgill chapel at Haugh Mill, so close to their home in Skyreholme, was the nearest place of worship of any persuasion.

Thomas's grand-daughter, Phyllis, has recalled how the early decades of the twentieth century were the most flourishing in the history of the chapel, due to interest taken by her influential family. [6] All the family worshipped there, and also their employees at the mill, together with many local farming families, each accompanied by their live-in farm labourers. Chapel anniversaries were always great social occasions, when local preachers and visiting choirs were entertained at Banquet House after the services. But, as the years went by, history repeated itself, and support for the chapel again faded, as it did for many others throughout the country.

Eventually, the Lumb family closed Skyreholme mill and moved from the area. Although other local families continued to support the chapel, membership continued to dwindle until, in the early 1990s, a decision was taken to close it, and it was converted into a private dwelling house.

Fn 1 Shoddy is shredded woollen waste.

References

1. Archive material from Grassington Methodist Chapel, Keighley Reference Library, and John Rylands Library, Manchester.

2. Survey of Howgill Chapel. No 52, Nov 1991, by members of the Vernacular Buildings Study Group, UWFS: Richard Bedford-Payne, Kurt and Jean Reinsch. Drawings Revised in January 2005 by Robert Mitchum (see Fig. 27).

3. Archive material.

4. ibid.

5. ibid.

6. Personal memories of Mrs Phyllis Dean (née Lumb) of Threshfield.

14. Dilemma for Duke and Parson: Barden, Chapel and Church

Brontë Bedford-Payne

The first Wesleyan Methodists had no chapel in Barden. Instead they occupied the building originally used for the Park School which in 1875 had moved to its present site nearer Barden Tower.

From a surviving letter, [1] it is apparent that by 1881 they had begun negotiations with the 8th Duke of Devonshire to obtain a suitable piece of land on which to build their own chapel. The tone of the letter reveals that the site chosen by the Duke for Wesleyan worship had been a matter of contention, and that the Minister presiding over the Grassington Circuit had been placed in what he referred to as *'an embarrassing position'* over the dispute.

To Gilson Martin,

Agent at Chatsworth for Spencer-Compton, 8th Duke of Devonshire.

19th October 1881

Sir,

Sometime ago I wrote to you respecting the piece of land which his Grace the Duke of Devonshire had selected for a Methodist Chapel at Barden. I pointed out the inconvenience of the situation, and on your declining to recommend a better site, according to promise, I communicated with His Grace in August last, asking him to reconsider the matter, and if there was no very strong objection against it, that he would grant us the site of the schoolroom we occupy, which in the judgement of all who know the case, is the best for our purpose.

Doubtless his Grace has intimated to you his decision, and I should esteem it a great favour, if you could help us in the matter by throwing some light on the subject. I am sorry to be obliged to trouble you so much, but I am placed in the most embarrassing position. I cannot positively decline the offer of His Grace, and I am equally bound not to accept the proposed site. Our people at Barden and in the Grassington Circuit decline to erect a chapel across the river and more than this, these gentlemen think they are not fairly dealt with.

They loyally supported the interests of His Grace during the last Election, and they may be asked to do so again, and now they are refused the small favour they ask. If they are not soon in possession of what they seek, I know how some of them will dispose of their voting power at a future date.

I hope, therefore, Sir, you may have the power to return a satisfactory reply to our request.

With Great Respect, I am, Sir, Yours Very Truly,

William Jones, Wesleyan Minister.

The 8th Duke was an active politician and leader of the Liberal party who, in 1880, had been asked by the Queen to form a government. [2] He would, perhaps, have been expected to take the request of his erstwhile voters seriously. The letter reflects a growing awareness of independence by the tenants on the Bolton Abbey estate, who realised the potential power of withholding political support for a candidate who they felt had treated them unfairly.

Fig. 30. Barden Bridge with Wesleyan Chapel on the hillside.

It is not known what site the Duke had in mind. The 1853 Ordnance Survey map shows a building named The Park School on School Brow, near to where the present chapel now stands. [3] The school is shown occupying a flat piece of land tucked into the corner wall of a field which, since the time of Lord Henry Clifford in the late 15th century, has been known as The Little Park. This platform of land on which the building stood can still be seen, and so can the track trodden by the feet of pupils who trudged from Barden Bridge through the wicket gate and up the hill to school. This must surely be the site of the schoolroom mentioned in William Jones' letter. However, it seems that the site for the chapel, favoured by 'our people at Barden and in the Grassington Circuit' was not granted, nor did they move across the river as the Duke suggested, the reasoning behind the final choice of site remaining a mystery (Fig. 30). The chapel has been built on an extremely steep slope, above living accommodation and a room known in the 20th century as 'the schoolroom'.

A flight of stone steps, hazardous and icy in winter, are located on the outside of the building, connecting the lower rooms with the chapel and the road. A similar example occurs at Hough Mill, where the Primitive Methodist Chapel is also squeezed between the road and a steeply rising hill, and in neither case was provision made for carriages to wait during services; it is almost as if the only land granted for the chapel was of no profitable use for the landlord and that very few concessions were made towards the needs of nonconformist worshippers.

Agreement having been achieved, the land was then leased for 99 years at a rent of 5 shillings per year and the chapel was built; one can still see within the porch a stone plaque commemorating its opening in 1885. The first Trustees included the tenants of nearby farms, John Ward Almack of Club Nook, John Atkinson of Low House Farm by Ghyll Beck, William Croft, a farmer and joiner from across the bridge at Holme Cottage and James Johnson, the reservoir keeper living at High Dock in Barden Great Park.

In 1892, a letter requesting assistance with the purchase of a harmonium was sent to the Duke of Devonshire for: *'we have a good choir who are wishful to obtain an instrument to help with the better rendering of the musical portions of the service'.* [4] The Duke, responded with a contribution of £2, and 24 other subscribers gave between half a crown and £1 each, 11 being residents of Barden, and the others living at Beamsley, Bolton Abbey, Burnsall and Appletreewick. Services continued to be held in the chapel until the late 1960s, and the schoolroom was much in demand for social occasions such as Sunday School teas, harvest suppers and shepherds' meetings. The Sabbath was strictly observed and for many families it would have seemed unthinkable not to attend chapel every Sunday; in any case, there was little else to do in most households, when secular activities such as playing games, knitting, pegging rugs or dressmaking were frowned upon.

When the river was not roaring down the valley in spate, families walking towards the chapel from their scattered homes on both sides of the valley could hear the shouts and songs of their neighbours and the sound of their boots ringing out on the hard surface of the road, while on dark winter evenings familiar clusters of lantern lights could be seen bobbing along the lanes leading from each of the farmhouses; during services these lanterns were extinguished and left in the chapel porch before being relit for the return home. During the Second World War, when oil and paraffin for the lamps were in short supply, and when blackout restrictions were strictly imposed, evening services and functions were often arranged to coincide with the full moon, so that people could find their way without the use of lamps.

Eventually, support for the chapel dwindled as Barden families found more freedom from the old Sunday conventions, and many were increasingly drawn to worship with a larger Wesleyan community, such as in the neighbouring village of Burnsall. The chapel became a private residence in 1969, with an art and craft shop selling only goods made in Yorkshire.

Anglicans attended services in the medieval chapel adjoining Barden Tower. This chapel was built in 1515 by Henry Clifford, known as 'the Shepherd Lord', to commemorate the victory of the battle of Flodden Field. It was then 'a chapelry of Skipton parish and its priest was appointed by Lord Henry' [5] who, as the 10th Lord Clifford of Skipton, already controlled the parish. After the Dissolution of Bolton Priory in 1539 the monastic estates passed into Clifford hands, [6] after which time Barden Chapel was served by the priest in charge of the Priory Church at Bolton.

From 1917-1954, services were conducted by the Reverend Cecil Tomlinson, Rector of Bolton Abbey, a well respected pastor who often cycled round his far flung parish to visit his flock. During his long incumbency he became an authority on local wildlife, being a keen and knowledgeable birdwatcher and possessing a notable collection of butterflies. Barden youngsters were encouraged to join the Bolton Abbey Choir, which meant long journeys down the dale after school in a horse drawn trap, packed tightly together under a weather-proof blanket. Childhood friendships formed here lasted a lifetime and former choristers, when they got together in later years told many tales of the happenings on choir outings in years gone by. They also recalled how decorating both chapels for festivals provided opportunities for socialising, when the gamekeeper's daughters from Drebley always brought large contributions of berried branches, mosses and primroses, found in remote places by their father. Ruth Lister who lived at Barden Tower enjoyed decorating the pulpit with holly for Christmas mornings: she said its prickles would keep the sermon short! For Easter, the girls gathered violets and wild daffodils from Springs Wood and took them round to housebound neighbours. Many headstones in the graveyard at Bolton Abbey are inscribed with familiar names associated with the farms in Barden: Demaine of Drebley and Barden Scale, Atkinson of Low House and Club Nook, Holmes and Holme of Drebley, Gamsworth and Hough Mill, Ward of Hough Mill and Holme Farm, Birch of Barden Low Reservoir and Club Nook, Ideson of Howgill and Gamsworth, Inman of Howgill and Drebley, Lister of Barden Tower and Watergate. From the Clifford papers formerly held in Skipton Castle, and now in the library of the Yorkshire Archaeological Society in Leeds, and from estate rentals held for the Trustees of the Chatsworth Estate at Bolton Abbey, it is known that generations of these families have leased the same farms since at least the early 17th century, when, in 1603 George Clifford, 3rd Earl of Cumberland issued them with leases. Now in the 21st century few of these family names survive, farm leases being less frequently passed down from one generation to another.

Services continued to be held at the ancient chapel attached to the Tower until the 1970s. It was closed in 1983, and has since become an echoing shell, stripped of its polished pews and ornaments of faith. Bolton Priory, 5 miles down the valley, now attracts a congregation which includes those from Barden whose forebears although baptised, married and buried there, could not have imagined regular church attendance at such a distance from their homes.

Sources:

Personal reminiscences of Dora Dunkley, daughter of Barden's schoolmistress, Betsy Inman and Gladys Chester (née Inman) gamekeeper's daughters, Ruth Lister, farmer's daughter, and Sidney Binns, whose father was an estate woodman.

References

1. Bolton MSS, Chatsworth Collection; Barden Township.
2. The Duchess of Devonshire (1982) The House. A Portrait of Chatsworth, London: Macmillan, p.3.
3. 1st edition Ordnance Survey map 1853.
4. Bolton MSS.
5. Spence, Richard (1994) The Shepherd Lord of Skipton Castle, Otley: Smith Settle.
6. Hamilton Thompson, A (1928) Bolton Priory History and Architecture, Thoresby Society Vol. XXX, Leeds: J. Whitehead and Son Ltd.

Industrial Archaeology

Linton Mill, the Tin Bridge and the River Wharfe

15. Corn To Textiles
Grassington Low Mill 1597-1995

Brontë Bedford-Payne

Grassington Low Mill dominates the local landscape on the north-east bank of the river Wharfe, about three hundred yards downstream from Linton Church, and above the stepping-stones. The mill, an imposing four storey building, rests on a substantial stone plinth arising from the river's edge, where an outcrop of Bowland Shale appears on the south side of the North Craven Fault.

Apart from the general architectural style and simplicity, some indications of the building's past can be seen: one is the open arch in the plinth, through which water which powered a wheel inside the building once spilled into the river below, another is the cascade of water pouring down the steep bank to enter the river upstream of the mill (Fig. 31).

There is both documentary and field evidence to show that over a period of centuries the powerful torrent of water issuing from a fissure known as Brow Well at the foot of the limestone hillside, at a temperature never lower than 90° centigrade, has long been used as a source of power. The stream was originally channelled towards a holding pond and dam from where it was released and controlled to turn water wheels belonging to an early corn mill, and later a

Fig. 31. Low Mill, early 1970s

textile mill. There was sufficient water to supply a second dam, which provided power to operate bellows for a lead smelt mill. The flow of water was unfailing in all weather conditions and this proved crucial in choosing the site for the mill. Water was the common factor running through centuries of change as social and economic conditions evolved and new enterprises and resources were developed and exploited.

The site is approached by means of a narrow walled lane branching off the road between Grassington and Hebden (Fig. 32). This lane has been enclosed from a broader hollow way, trodden over a long period of time by the hooves of laden packhorses, the wheels of carts and the heavy boots and clogs of people who toiled up and down from Grassington; it descends steeply, passing between Brow Well and two former dams (Fig. 33). One of these has now been filled in to form a garden and the other holds tanks for a trout hatchery.

The earliest surviving records date from the 1590s, when George Clifford, 3rd Earl of Cumberland, was Lord of the Manor of Grassington. (Appendix B.1.)

Fig. 32. Low Mill from Low Mill Lane
Christopher P. Payne 1987

These records establish that this was the site of the medieval soke mill [Fn1] owned by the Earl, to whom all manorial tenants owed suite and service. [Fn2]

They paid all the usual multure tolls, [Fn1] whereby tenants contributed a share towards any necessary repairs to the mill, and all their corn, peas and beans had to be taken there to be ground. In 1597 a reference to the mill appears in an indenture of mortgage drawn up between the Earl and a tenant Thomas Hewitt, in which 'suite and service at the Lord's Mill'[1] was mentioned. In 1603, the Pierse Survey of Grassington tenants and their holdings names the Earl's brother, Francis Clifford, as holding one half of the mill, and Robert Oglethorpe as leaseholder of the other half.

Fn1. Soke is derived from the Old English 'soc', medieval Latin 'soca' meaning a right of local jurisdiction. The tenant of a soke mill was a socman. The soke of a mill included the Lord of the Manor's right to prevent any other mill being built in the same manor, and the power to compel the tenants of the manor to grind their corn at the soke mill. The Lord of the Manor owned the mill.

Fn2. Suite and service at the mill included maintenance of the dam and the mill house, and the cost of carriage of the millstones.

A separate rental, also dated 1603, also refers to him as the leaseholder. Some time after 1605 , when the 4th Earl, Francis Clifford, had succeeded his brother, the mill became an ordinary property on the market, and so was no longer a soke mill subject to the Lord of the Manor.

Despite this the deeds relating to the mill dated 1742, 1747, 1749, 1769, and 1772 contain clauses which refer to 'all manner of multure tolls, soke suite etc.' [2] as used

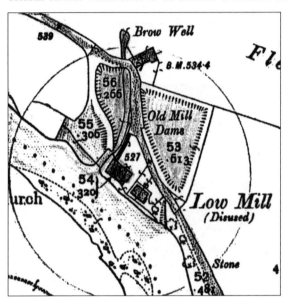

Fig. 33. Brow Well, the Dams and Low Mill

in the days of the old manorial system. From the time of the earliest deed the names of people who leased or owned the mill appear in the records. Thomas Hewitt in 1590, William Stockdale in 1743, William Wrathall in 1747, and Thomas Craven in 1782, are names associated with long-established families in Grassington, Linton, Threshfield, and Burnsall.

Later in the eighteenth century, merchants from further afield, from Knaresborough, Kildwick near Keighley, and Stanley near Wakefield, exchanged sales and mortgages. In 1776 the property described as *'all that water corn-mill in Grassington with the Drying Corn Kiln therewith now used and late in the possession of Henry Wrathall and now of Wm. Bradfield'* [3] was transferred to William Bradfield of Killinghall and Jane Buck of Knaresborough. These transactions suggest that as the eighteenth century progressed and the old manorial tolls and monopolies were discarded, trade spread beyond the immediate locality of a small, semi-feudal community.

A major factor contributing to the demise of the Grassington corn mill was the establishment in 1750 of a Turnpike Trust between Grassington, Pateley Bridge and Knaresborough.

Fn1. Multure tolls were payments in kind to the miller and consisted of grain or flour.

Turnpikes sought to address the problems caused by inadequate maintenance of roads, which had resulted in a network of quagmires, impassable for wheeled carts and wagons. In 1758 revenue was raised for drainage and repair and also to construct new causeways in order to open a turnpike road, on which tolls were collected.

This road not only opened up trade between Grassington and the flourishing markets in Ripon and Knaresborough, but it also enabled abundant supplies of corn to be transported to the upper Dales; corn grown in the fertile Vale of York where the climate and the land were more favourable for arable crop, and where much of it was milled before dispatch.

A small water mill was not likely to be a profitable long-term investment under these conditions and Low Mill went into decline. By the 1790s, grinding of corn had ceased, and a new industrial opportunity emerged: mechanised cotton-spinning, made possible by the invention of Hargreave's spinning jenny in 1764, Arkwright's spinning frame in 1767, and Crompton's 'mule' in 1775. In 1785 Arkwright's patents lapsed, leading to a surge in the establishment of water-powered textile mills on the banks of nearly every possible tributary stream in the Penines. The site by Brow Well must have seemed ideal: a site where corn milling and lead smelting were in decline, and where the constant flow of water would provide sufficient power to meet the increased demands of machinery for spinning cotton.

At the same time as the effects of the Industrial Revolution were being felt at Low Mill, the lives of miners and other small holders were profoundly affected by a series of Parliamentary Enclosure Acts, whereby local landowners were empowered to divide and enclose hitherto common pastures. In 1788 a survey was made in Grassington and a map drawn, and on 1st May 1792 a Commissioners' Award allowed *'the inclosing of the several stinted pastures called Old Pasture, New Pasture, Botton, and Losssgill Bank in the Township of Grassington, in the County of York'*. In the years that followed, and in common with other landless labourers throughout the nation, many village families, who had hitherto been dependent on the commons and on their smallholdings to supplement their meagre living, found themselves denied their means of subsistence. Now, the able bodied wives and children of the miners constituted a ready labour force for the cotton mills newly operating in Linton, Threshfield and Grassington. The names of these villagers, appearing as they do in the parish registers, [4] are listed with indications of some occupations, but it is not possible to ascertain which individuals worked at which mill.

During this time of great change, it is not entirely clear what happened to Low Mill. Possibly the old corn-mill, with its gable-end wheel housed externally in the pit adjacent to the waterfall, was demolished, or, more probably, was used as foundations for the new mill then built to house machinery for spinning cotton.

We can infer this from field observations and photographs of the present building, dating from before major alterations took place in the 1970s. The plinth on which the building stands is the foundation for the initial three-storey mill dating from the 1790s [5] Study of the arrangement of the windows on the river frontage reveals a blank space at ground level, above the arched opening for the tailrace, indicating the position of the wheelhouse. Window openings on the first and second floors show that an upper floor ran over the wheelhouse. Such arrangements were

common in Yorkshire cotton mills. [6] The wheelhouse is still in place, now containing a staircase leading up from the ground floor, the former entry point for the water being marked by a stone lined cavity in the wall half way up the stairs. The goit is now filled in to form an approach to the house, but careful inspection of the stonemasonry of the retaining wall (Fig. 34a & 34b) shows the north wall of a stone goit or channel, built on a wider stone plinth. Water from the dam was led along this channel to enter the wheelhouse at a point below the modern doorway. The water channel entered the wheelhouse at a point level with the centre of the wheel, which implies it would have been a breast shot wheel. Drawings and measurements suggest it could have been no more than 15 feet in diameter. (Appendix B.2 Les. Bloom).

Fig. 34a. The wall of the 18th Century Goit after alterations 1975

The coming of the textile industry to the Dales only became feasible after the provision of adequate means of communication such as turnpike roads and inland waterways. The Leeds and Liverpool canal opened in Skipton in 1773 and in Gargrave in 1777, linking the great industrial centres in West Yorkshire and Lancashire with the scattered mills of Craven. This canal provided a way for goods to be transported by horse drawn barge rather than as before by packhorse. From then on the narrow winding road which led from Gargrave to Grassington was improved and maintained by successive Dukes of Devonshire, primarily for the transport of lead from Grassington Moor, where the Burlingtons and later the Cavendish family, direct descendants of the Clifford Lords, had retained their mineral rights. The lack of a toll bar and milestones indicate this was never a turnpike road. It is bordered in part by hedges, partly by stone wall; there are no wide verges as it wends it way up hill and down dale, following ancient, sinuous field boundaries. It passes in hollow ways between the estates of Eshton and Flasby before reaching Hetton and diverging to Rylstone, where, from the 1790s onwards, cotton mills existed in both villages.

At the height of the lead mining industry there would have been a constant stream of packhorse trains passing to and from the wharves in Gargrave, carrying cotton, wool and other merchandise to and from the textile mills in Wharfedale as well lead and coal. An entry appearing in the parish register for November 24th 1765, throws another light on the nature of traffic along this road: *'William Gibson, a native of Ginea or a Negreo slave were baptised by me, Benj. Smith, B.D. Rector.'* [7]

This is a reminder that, with the import of sugar and cotton through Liverpool, there also came slaves, who would pass with their English masters along the canal systems into remote valleys of Northern England.

The textile industry in the district was started in the 1790s by John, William and George Birkbeck, members of a Quaker family in Settle. They were prosperous merchant bankers who owned Grassington Low Mill, Linton Mill and Scawgill. The date when they acquired Low Mill is not known, because records lodged at the Yorkshire Archaeological Society cease after 1782, and those found in the Land Tax Assessment do not begin until 1830. [8] Between these years Low Mill again underwent major structural alterations, changing from spinning cotton to spinning worsted. [Fn1]

Further study of the frontage shown on the pre-1970s photograph (see Fig. 31) shows where a third floor was added and the roof of the mill was raised. There are changes in the style of the building above the second floor where the stonework of the walls, the window surrounds, the size of the quoins, the style of the roof-kneelers, and the presence of sack hoists and 'taking in doors' are characteristic of an early nineteenth century textile mill.

It is recognisable as such to the present day, despite the changes wrought since the building lost its industrial identity.

Birkbeck and Co. continued to spin worsted at Low Mill. In 1837, their manager was William Wall, who may have been the first occupant of the cottage built on a separate plinth adjoining the mill.

In 1847 the railway from Leeds and Bradford reached Skipton, and in 1853 a section of the road between Cracoe and Skipton was made into a turnpike, opening a more direct route from Grassington to the railway.

Later, a through line was opened between Skipton and the West Riding, Manchester and Liverpool, and from this time onwards trade with Knaresborough and Ripon by the old turnpike road through Pateley Bridge declined.

The focus then shifted towards the markets in Skipton and centres of the woollen

Fn1 Worsted is a fine smooth yarn spun from combed long staple wool.

trade such as Bradford and Halifax.

On May 16th 1856, following the deaths of the Birkbeck brothers, their Trustees sold the mill by auction. It was advertised as:

'Lot 6... and also all that mill called Grassington Low Mill, situated at Grassington about 9 miles from Skipton, now in the occupation of Messrs. Spencer and Co. as tenants thereof and used as a worsted mill, together with a water wheel which is 10 horse power, the dam and appurtenances thereof. The supply of water is regular and abundant.' [10]

The purchaser was Henry Alcock, a Skipton merchant and local landowner, who also owned Grassington House. He installed Joseph Spencer as his manager. Between 1878 and 1894, the mill was owned by John Holdsworth and Co. Ltd., worsted spinners of Shaw Lodge Mills, Shibden Dale, Halifax, and occupied by successive members of the Holdsworth family.

'In 1900 Clement Holdsworth, from his considerable personal wealth, purchased the estate at Scargill near Kettlewell, where he sustained a lifestyle as a country gentleman, shooting grouse on Conistone moor and fishing for trout in the Wharfe. He eventually bought the small mansion Netherside Hall, and he moved there in 1912.' [11]

The Holdsworths were the last worsted manufacturers to use the mill. It then became unoccupied and fell into disuse for some time. However, a variety of small industries were set up after the turn of the century, continuing to exploit the site and the source of waterpower.

Fig. 34b. Site of Goit at Low Mill Northallerton PRO. Date unknown

There is some evidence from the Factory Returns [12] that silk was manufactured here, and in 1908, Joseph Barker capitalised on one of the waste products of the woollen industry, lanolin, and made soap. While all this was happening to the mill, conveyances were being drawn up on behalf of the 9th Duke of Devonshire for the sale of the two mill dams, one of which had been associated with the smelt-mill (Fig. 35).

These transactions are reminders that the ancient mineral rights were still being exercised at the end of the nineteenth century. In 1895, the dams came into the hands of Ralph Bowdin

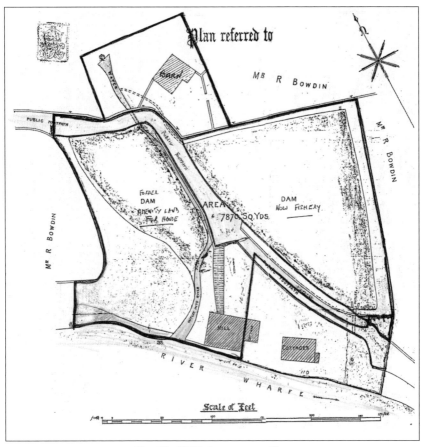

Fig. 35. 1905 Conveyance Plan

of Hebden, and in 1905 they were sold to Septimus Wray for £450.

In the 1930s, Marie Hartley and Ella Pontefract described how they saw the mill whilst writing their book Wharfedale:

> *'The old Grassington soke mill stands on the beck, deserted now, its vacant windows looking tragically out upon a scene in which it no longer has a part'* [13]

By the mid-twentieth century, the building was owned by Harry Binns, a poulterer and game merchant of Grassington, who installed a small wheel brought from the mill at Hartlington in order to power a wood-turning lathe. The Binns family raised chickens and pigs in and around the premises until, in the 1970s, a demolition order was placed on the building. It was then sold to a builder trading under the name *'Your Cottage in the Country'*, who converted it into a private house.

Shortly after this, the flow of water from Brow Well was directed to supply a modern rainbow trout hatchery within the original holding pond.

This is still in operation, and from here some brown trout fingerlings are also raised to restock the Wharfe, perhaps replacing those originally fished when corn was ground in a hand quern, centuries before the first water wheel was turned.

Sources

Susan D Brooks: unpublished papers relating to Low Mill
The Tithe Award for Grassington (1846)
Census Returns for Grassington (1851)
Raistrick, Arthur 1967 Old Yorkshire Dales Newton Abbott., David and Charles
Ingle, George (1997) Yorkshire Cotton Preston, Carnegie Publishing Ltd.
Graham Shutt: extracts from thesis 1979 Wharfedale Water Mills

Acknowledgements

Leslie Bloom, for references to the Holdsworth family.
Ruth Camm, for contributions to the script of this article.
Arnold Pacey, Yorkshire Vernacular Buildings Study Group, for comments regarding the position of the wheel, and the dating of the present building at Low Mill.

References

1   Brooks, Susan (1975) Collected Papers, unpublished, see Appendix 1.
2   ibid.
3   ibid.
4   The Parish Registers for Linton-in-Craven Vol. I (1562-1779), Vol. II. (1779-1812).
5   Raistrick, Arthur (1972) Industrial Archaeology London: Eyre and Methuen.
6   Giles, Collum and Goodall (1992) Yorkshire Textile Mills London: Royal Commission for Historical Monuments.
7   The Registers of the Parish Church of Linton-in-Craven Vol. I (1562-1779). Edited by the Rev. F.A.C. Shore.
8   Brooks 1975.
9   Joy, David (2002) Hebden The History of a Township Skipton: Hebden History Group.
10 Brooks 1975.
11 Holdsworth, Dina Maria (2002) 200 Years in the Textile Industry: Short Company History Halifax: John Holdsworth & Co Ltd.
12 Shutt, Graham (1979) Wharfedale Water Mills, Unpublished Thesis for M. Phil., University of Leeds.
13 Pontefract, Ella and Hartley, Marie (1937) Wharfedale London: Dent and Son.

16. The Earl's Sumpter Pots –
Lead Smelting by Brow Well 1605-1793

Ruth Camm

Long before the end of the 16th century, like other great landlords of the time, the Cliffords were keen to exploit the mineral resources on their estates. George Clifford, third Earl of Cumberland, was drawn into iron and lead mining activities by his more enterprising and profit-motivated wife Margaret; but the initiative for developing the lead-mining and smelting at Grassington came from George's brother Francis, who succeeded as fourth Earl in 1605. Coal was being mined in Craven, iron in the Forest of Knaresborough and there were ironworks and a hammer forge at Crimple near Spofforth. The coal, iron and lead would supply their own considerable needs, but the estates needed profitable, long-term sources of income to supplement the revenue from their rents, which could not be increased easily.

By 1559 the Cliffords had acquired the manor of Grassington, and owned the mineral rights, but their leasehold and freehold tenants had rights of turbary, [Fn1] so that peat could not legitimately be used as a fuel in the lead-smelting process. It had been known from Roman times that there were lead deposits on Grassington Moor and there is evidence of small-scale mining there before the end of the sixteenth century: the remains of bell pits [Fn2] and the bole hills [Fn3] used for smelting survive.

Having decided to build a lead smelting mill which would be more efficient in its use of fuel than the bole hills, Francis was faced with what would now be called a logistical problem: the lead was on (or in) Grassington Moor, where there was no reliable water power, timber for fuel would come, initially at least, from Grass Wood, and the best source of water power was near the Grassington bank of the River Wharfe, at the site of the Earl's manorial corn mill. He chose to build the smelt mill there, a few yards upstream from the corn mill, and the water from the underground spring at Brow Well provided the power for both mills.

Fn1. Turbary is the right to cut peat for fuel on common ground, or on ground owned by another person.
Fn2. Bell pits were shallow bell shaped workings strung out along over outcropping veins of lead.
Fn3. Bole hills: places where in ancient times lead ores were smelted.

The smelt mill was built in 1605. Very little remains of the building, but there is slag on the ground above the river bank.

The furnace, or ore hearth, was built to a design patented by William Humphrey in 1565, and used extensively in Derbyshire.

Essentially it was a box built of firestones round three sides and open at the front. The ore hearth was surmounted by a chimney with open arches at the front and sides to allow the smelters access to the fire. The positioning of the furnace and the pair of large bellows in their timber framework would be dictated by the siting of the water wheel outside the building, with the wheel's axle working the bellows. The smelt mill was large enough to accommodate the much later additions of two more ore hearths, requiring a second water wheel and another chimney.

It appears that smelting was initially carried out without a chimney, for 2 tons of lead were sold by the Earl's agent in 1606, and it was not until August 1607 that Peter and Henry Stott spent over a fortnight walling the first chimney. The normal pattern was for the chimney to rise 12 feet above the roof, but even so there must have been considerable atmospheric pollution, with people and grazing animals affected, not to mention the two smelters. At the base of the ore hearth and projecting in front of it was a cast iron receptacle called the workstone. This was heated with fuel from the fire in preparation for the molten lead which ran along a groove into a pan connected to the workstone. From here the molten lead ran into the sumpter pot, which was a cast iron basin about 17 inches in diameter.

Wood for the furnace was dried in large bowl-shaped kilns, the remains of which can still be found in Grass Wood. These were up to 15 feet in diameter and 10 feet deep, with a lining of paving-stones and a sloping entrance along one side. The wood, stripped of its bark and chopped into pieces about 6 inches long and 4 inches square in section, was thrown onto a timber grid through which heat from a slow fire below penetrated to extrude the sap from the chopwood - known as white coal because of its final appearance. Towards the end of the 17th century, coal which had been mined on Thorpe Fell and at Bordley was used to supplement depleted reserves of wood, but the proportion of coal had to be limited, to prevent impurities like sulphur affecting the quality of the lead. To give some idea of the wood-coal proportions: in 1701-2, 124 loads of coal were used with 432 loads of chopwood when about 60 tons of lead was produced.

One firing of the furnace could produce 4-5 cwt. of lead and a full day's shift 2-3 tons. The ore hearth was filled with layers of fuel alternating with a mixture of slag cinders, partly smelted ore from a previous firing, and lime, used as a flux. The dressed ore was place on top and allowed to 'roast' to remove moisture before being stirred with long pokers into the hottest part of the fire. A pair of bellows made of hide pumped air alternately through apertures at the back of the ore hearth. This was done by means of two pawls or cams fixed to the rotating axle of the water wheel, each in turn depressing an arrangement of wooden bars which squeezed air out of the bellows. Release of the bars was regulated by a vertical cable attached to a higher horizontal bar with a counterweight.

The two smelters stirred the fire to encourage every part of the ore to give up its molten lead rather than letting it evaporate into the chimney or condense in a solid mass. As the molten lead collected in the sumpter pot, one of the smelters poured the lead into moulds, using a long-handled ladle which held about 4 stones of lead, while the other smelter cleared away the cinders which had been sucked into the muzzles of the bellows. At Grassington Low Mill, each piece of lead weighed 123 lbs. and 20 pieces made a ton. Each piece was stamped with a letter which was changed after every 400 pieces.

It was customary to resmelt the slag when the work of smelting the dressed ore was completed, producing 'slaglead'. A hotter fire was required, and charcoal provided this.

The total lead production at Low Mill in each of the years 1612 and 1613 was about 19 tons. A slightly later experiment with a parcel of ore weighing 4 cwt. 3st. 10lbs. from a mill at Thieveley in Lancashire produced 2 cwt. 7 st. 7lbs. of lead. Low Mill's was a good result compared with what Thieveley mill was obtaining using foot-bellows. The figures indicate that Low Mill was producing lead weighing 67% of the weight of ore being smelted. Even so, this meant that for every 20 tons of lead produced, over 6 tons of slag had to be disposed of.

The number of days on which smelting took place in 1612 and 1613 were ten and sixteen respectively. Lead mining was a by-employment for the miners at this time. Their numbers varied between 12 and 20, in loose partnerships of two or three. As smallholders or general labourers they were occupied at lambing, shearing and harvest-time. It was imperative for landless wage-labourers, often earning less than one shilling per day, to find other sources of income to avoid the need for parish relief.

However, miners' wages of about 1s.2d. per day did not provide an incentive for greater productivity, nor were their jobs secure until circa 1617, when Earl Francis changed the rules and leased his mines to the miners.

Until then, the Earl had paid all the wages, the cost of upkeep and repairs to the mill, provided the fuel and supplied timber for the mines and the miners' huts. Here they stored their tools and stockpiled the dressed ore until they had enough to make a worthwhile journey by packhorse to the smelt mill. A normal load for each animal was 2¼ cwt.

The Earl's costs in 1612 and 1613 were £110 and £115, including £2 for tithes to the Rector of Linton and 6s. 8d. for tithes to the Rector of Kettlewell. Total profit in these two years was £57 and £75; the lead was sold at £9 per ton and then the price rose to £9 10s.

In the early years of the 17th century Francis used some of his lead for repairs to the roof at Barden Tower, and also at Skipton Castle after a chimney blew down. Repairs renovations at the castle made steady demands: a new roof on the dining chamber and lead fall-pipes at the gatehouse, while in the 1630s, three loads of lead were taken to his mansion at Londesborough for the construction of a conduit to the house laundry from a stream in the village. The Earl's lead was used to reline tan pits at Bolton, and in 1638 three tons were sent to Carlisle Castle which was being restored by Francis, who was its governor. On a much smaller scale, the gamekeepers made lead shot for the guns.

In these ways, as well as financially, the Earl's coal, iron and lead mining and smelting enterprises helped to support the family's aristocratic lifestyle. As his mining interests spread into Westmorland he decided to cut his expenditure on wages by leasing his mines. The effect in Grassington was a steady increase in output, for now the miners had an incentive as well as greater security of tenure. They would own two thirds of the lead they produced, while the Lord of the Manor retained one third as duty. In 1630 Francis made a net profit of £232 4s. 11d. He built a second smelt mill near Coalgrove Beck on the High Moor, and because of greatly extended mining there, both mills worked to their full capacity.

In the years leading up to the Civil War, the annual output of lead averaged 70 tons, so that 20 miners and their working families had between them 46 tons, giving an income of roughly £20 per family. Not every year was prosperous, but when the miners received their 'pays' there would be immediate claims on their sudden riches. A pair of men's boots cost about 8s. 0d. and a 'suit of cloth' up to 15s. 0d. A shovel cost about 2s.4d. Ale was 1d. a quart.

Of the 22 miners and smelters in 1642, some were the second generation of miners who had come 37 years earlier from Derbyshire; the rest were local men. The thrifty ones became more prosperous, buying the old fee farmsFn1 from the Lord of the Manor and trying to increase their land holding. They requested a formal meeting, called the Barmoot Court, to set down laws and customs to protect themselves and when disputes arose, and to record earlier agreements made with Earl Francis about his responsibilities. By 1642, Frances Clifford had died, and his son Henry succeeded to the Earldom. The new 5th Earl of Cumberland granted their request, and the Court was held in the presence of the barmaster Peter Pulman, the Earl's agent, and the deputy barmaster George Smith, the miners' representative.

The latter was a 3rd generation Grassington blacksmith, and likely to have been a smelter.

Here are two of the twenty laws recorded.

'18. Item. Wee set Downe that when their is a new workestone laid it shall have the

Fn1. Fee farms: farms for which some service is paid to the Lord of the Manor.

pan fild at my Lord's Charg with lead according to former custom and everie man to leave it as full as he findes it in painer of 6s.8d.

19. Item. Wee set Downe that the smelters shall be Chosen one by the Consent of the barmaister and the other by the Jurie.'

There was also a law to ensure the barmaster 'Keep true and lawfull weights at the melne and not to alter them to wrong the myners.'

Of the 5 miners who failed to appear at the barmoot court, 2 were fined (6d. and 2d.) and 3 were pardoned. The court also dealt with infringements of the laws. The barmaster weighed and kept records of all the lead produced and collected the 'lot' for the Lord of the Field. [Fn1] The miners tried to avoid paying their duty, and their proportion of lead fell to two fifths in the 1690s and one sixth in the 1770s.

A barmaster called George Bradley said, when he took up his post in 1764, 'All the smelting mills lay open and the lessees of each mine took a quantity of lead for their own use, and not one pound of lead paid or received for duty.' Locks were put on the doors, but determined thieves broke into the mill at night. The barmaster apparently persuaded the culprits to see the error of their ways. Although throughout the two centuries of lead mining and smelting at Grassington, discontent and controversy arose frequently, the miners' grievances do not appear to have been about the dreadful working conditions but about the payment of duty lead and having to buy wood for the mines. They came into conflict with other miners when boundaries were crossed, usually underground, or when a miner caused water from his mine to enter another's. During the Civil War some of the Derbyshire miners returned home, and for a time Low Mill suffered a setback, both through a shortage of workmen and of wood for fuel.

The 5th Earl of Cumberland died in 1643, after only one year in office, and the second Earl of Cork, brother to Robert Boyle, the 'father of chemistry', became Lord of the Manor after inheriting Clifford estates through his marriage to Earl Henry's daughter, Elizabeth Clifford.

In 1651 the barmaster Humphrey Hughes tried to keep lead production going by finding a new source of timber at Threshfield. He paid Thorpe men by allowing his workmen to take hearthstones from Thorpe Fell, and he came to a new arrangement with the miners about timber: they now had to pay for it. The miners objected and stopped work for almost two years. In a sense this was a watershed in the development of mining and smelting in the area.

Fn1 After the Dissolution much of the ore bearing ground formerly owned by the monasteries was confiscated by the Crown. It was subsequently sold or leased to private individuals, who were known as Lords of the Field. They, in turn, allowed smaller parties to work for lead, but demanded that they should assign to them a certain proportion of the smelted ore.

Water was indeed a problem in the neglected mine workings, and Hughes drew up a 21 year lease for 4 partners prepared to invest £400 in reclamation work and the construction of a sough [Fn1] to drain a wide area of the moor. The Corks (now Burlingtons) agreed to contribute to the cost: they raised the money from the sale of duty lead, which had now been reduced to one quarter. Production of lead at the mill returned to pre-civil war levels. George Smith, assistant barmaster, recorded repairs to the lead mill's chimney, bellows and dam in 1658 at a total cost of £1 19s. John Lupton and partners chopped and dried sufficient wood to smelt 20 tons of lead for £7 10s.

Outlets for the lead were not very different from those in earlier decades: repairs at Newbiggin and Bolton Hall, and the Burlington residences; also, Lady Anne Clifford bought more lead for Barden Tower and replaced the 44 tons stripped from Skipton Castle by the Parliamentary army. The last half of the 17th century and the first decades of the eighteenth were marked by a steady increase in mining and smelting operations, with investors either contracting miners or employing them as wage labour.

The landowners clung to their mineral rights, and these were passed through marriage along a line of Burlingtons to the Devonshires. In 1703 a large area of Grassington moor was opened up for exploration after Jane, the Countess Dowager of Bridgewater, (who leased veins from the Earl of Burlington) had been persuaded to remove restrictions on prospecting, as well as removing a levy of 12s. per ton on the miners' smelted lead. Now the duty was to be further reduced to one fifth.

In spite of a climate of continuing contention and disputes, output rose from about 100 tons in 1700 to 450 tons in 1752 and by 1765 began to reach more than 500 tons. A second ore hearth was installed at Low Mill in 1741, and a new wheel replaced the old one, while in 1756 a new smelt mill was built on Grassington Moor to meet the required smelting capacity. Now there were six ore hearths, three at each mill.

The mill on the moor and the third hearth at Low Mill were installed at the expense of the Coalgrovehead Company, formed about 1750, but the 4th Duke of Devonshire reimbursed them later: he clearly wished to retain ownership.

The Company smelted their ore at Low Mill; so did James Swale and Co. who mined the Ripley vein and Robert Pickles and Co. of the 'Blew Levell' mine.

At 5 o'clock one morning in August 1774, George Bradley the barmaster was awakened with the news that Low Mill was in flames.

The response was rapid, for although the fire destroyed the front of the mill and damaged the roof, as well as melting 540 pieces of lead stored in the building, 70 pieces were resmelted that morning. The cost of repairing the damage was £8 13 6d, less £8 0s. 0d. for roof repairs already planned.

Fn1 Sough: drainage channel.

The barmaster thought the fire had been caused by the smelters not properly extinguishing the fires at the end of the previous day's shift. In spite of the smelt mill's continuing efficiency - it now had a second water wheel - the writing was on the wall. Output from the mines fell during the 1780's to about 300 tons in 1790. Fuel supplies were critically low, and the supply of peat from the moor was restricted. In 1792 the problems were solved when the new Cupola Mill on the edge of Grassington High Moor began smelting. It had two reverberatory furnaces which burned coal – with this process the ore did not come into contact with the coal. The last smelting at Low Mill was in February 1793.

The demise of the smelt mill after nearly two centuries of life, and the building of the Cupola, marked the creation of a new era of lead mining on Grassington Moor. In 1792 the 5th Duke of Devonshire financed the excavation of a deep drainage level linked to individual mineshafts; lead mining companies began to invest in mechanisation including winding gear, grinding mills and pumping devices. Water power on an extensive scale was made available by the construction of a new watercourse system. It was all part of the opening chapter of the industrial revolution, and so was the transformation which took place at Low Mill at the same time. The corn mill and the smelt mill made way for a cotton spinning mill and it is reasonable to assume that they provided at least the foundation stones for the new building. The many generations of people who provided their skills and hard labour for little reward had enabled all these industrial activities to succeed in their turn. They did so in part because working people had adapted to changes in employment patterns just as readily as their lords and masters had been keen to profit from the latest economic enterprises.

Sources:

Raistrick, Arthur and Jennings, Bernard (1965) A History of Lead Mining in the Pennines, London: Longmans, Green & Company Ltd.

Raistrick, Arthur (1973) Lead Mining in the Mid-Pennines, Truro: D. Bradford Barton Ltd.

Spence, Richard T. (1992) Mining and Smelting in Yorkshire by the Clifford Earls of Cumberland, in the Tudor and Early Stuart Period. Yorkshire Archaeological Journal. Vol. 64.

Clough, Robert T. (1962) The Lead Smelting Mills of the Yorkshire Dales, Leeds: Published by the Author.

Gill, M.C., (1993) The Grassington Mines, Northern Mines Research Association.

The prices of goods quoted were taken from a comprehensive list made in Southampton in 1625, the first year of the reign of Charles 1 and prepared for Hugh May, the Clerk of the Markets to His Majesty's Household. He was paid 1s.1d. per day.

The list was obtained from http:/www.portsdowndemon.co.uk/mark.htm

17. The Enigma of Scaw Ghyll –
Tracing the History of a Water Mill

Philip Sugden

The purpose of this exercise was to try to decipher the history of the author's house, Scaw Ghyll, Grassington, by looking at the structure of the present building and also by examining such written sources as exist, both published and unpublished. Several individuals have already looked at this question but with results which were both inconclusive and inconsistent. I have drawn extensively on this earlier research and commented on it where appropriate. The principal documentary source that these earlier studies drew upon was the early title deeds of the property, which have passed into the ownership of the writer. Throughout I have used the present spelling of Scaw Ghyll; this appears to have been a 20th century poetic change with early records referring to Scaw Gill.

Local folklore says that the building, which is now a single dwelling house, had been a manorial soke mill, a cotton mill, a butter factory and two or more cottages. None of the earlier studies of the house provided explanations that are wholly consistent with either the present building or the historical record. This paper critically assesses these earlier studies in order to try and reach a more robust explanation of this enigmatic building.

The house is in two halves, each with its own pitched roof and joined by a small central passage running the length of the property. The rear (eastern) part of the property shows clear evidence of having started life as a barn or similar industrial premises whilst the front portion appears to be a conversion of three modest cottages. This was the easy explanation of the building's layout that was given to the writer when the property was acquired. Members of the Vernacular Buildings Group of the Upper Wharfedale Field Society, who measured the building on 6th March 1997, also accepted this and reported as follows (Fig. 36 & 37):

There was probably an earlier building on this site, which was used as a corn mill, very likely being the most northerly building in the old Saxon town. The earliest references to the present building were in 1729. This is probably the approximate date of the present structure, which, judging from the thickness of certain of the internal walls, started its life as two separate buildings; a mill to the east and a block of cottages a few feet away to the west. Initially the industrial part was used as a cotton worsted spinning mill'. [1]

There are however two important clues associated with this report: one is the statement that *'The stone surrounds to the kitchen window and the bedroom window above are probably late 19th century'*, and the other is the observation that only one half of the building appeared on the First Edition Ordinance Survey Map. [2] I will return to these points when looking at the dating the eastern half of the property.

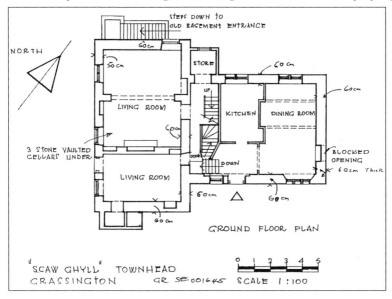

Fig. 36. Plan of Scaw Ghyll

There is no documentary evidence of a corn mill existing at Scaw Ghyll in either the present building or in an earlier building on the site.

This was the view of Arthur Raistrick who, as reported by the following two independent sources, believed that Grassington may originally have been divided into two manors with Scaw Ghyll being one of the two manorial soke mills: Mr Richard Harland of Grassington reported having heard this at a lecture delivered by Dr Raistrick to the Workers Education Association, and the papers of Miss Susan Brooks also attributed this interpretation of Scaw Ghyll to Dr Raistrick. However, Miss Brooks was dismissive of this theory because Scaw Ghyll was not shown in the Grassington manorial records of 1603 and because the other mill had sufficient capacity. Neither point addressed the issue of two manors.

The question of whether Scaw Ghyll was ever a corn mill is total speculation since no written or archaeological evidence exists. The most compelling argument is that Scaw Ghyll can be dated to 1729 and cotton spinning was not introduced to the area until about 1790 so the building must have had some alternative use for the first 60 years. George Ingle wrote that

'In the Dales large numbers of corn mills came onto the market following the changes in agriculture at the end of the 18th century... It is possible to find several of the early mills which were built on the corn mill sites. It is interesting to speculate that Scaw Ghyll may be one such'. [3]

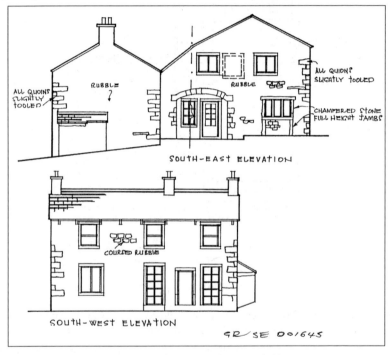

Fig. 37. Elevations of Scaw Ghyll

The primary source of evidence for this use was found in an abstract of the title to the property dated 1857: this traced its ownership and use from 1729 to that date. There is also an underground stream adjacent to the property and limited archaeological evidence of a wheel pit. The title documents show that Scaw Ghyll was in the ownership of Thomas Lupton, yeoman, and his successors from 1729 until 1819, though the property was the subject of a complex series of mortgages and leases between those dates. The period during which it was used as a cotton mill was brief, perhaps from 1792 to 1812. The mill was first operated by a partnership between Moses Wright and William Hardacre from about 1792 until their partnership was dissolved in 1809. There were brief attempts to operate the mill by William Gill and then by Richard Chester before it was converted into cottages. An indenture dated 1810 refers to:

'All that piece or parcel of land ... Commonly known by the name of Scaw Gill with the building or edifice therein situate formerly occupied as a mill or factory by Mr Samuel Gill, lately by Richard Chester but now converted into two messuages or dwelling houses' [4]

When the building was advertised for sale in the Halifax Journal on 28th June 1813 it was described as having been recently converted to cottages but easily capable of being converted back to a mill.

Operating small mills in the Grassington area appears to have been a hazardous financial affair and the complex mortgages which affected Scaw Ghyll were by no means unique. Samuel Gill also leased Linton Mill together with a partner, James Parker of Gargrave. Mr Parker also owned Hebden Mill prior to becoming bankrupt in 1811. In 1819 the last of the Luptons, John, emigrated to the United States and the property passed to a consortium including the Birkbeck family who already owned larger mills at Grassington and Linton.

It is not clear why the Birkbecks came to own Scaw Ghyll, possibly to shut out competition, but more probably by default as mortgagers. John Peart, gentleman of Settle, who was described as a trustee of the Birkbecks, seems to have been the occupier and part owner along with a number of other Birkbeck connections. In 1856 the Birkbecks offered a number of fields in Grassington and Linton for sale by public auction in the Devonshire Hotel, Grassington. Lot 5 comprised *'Those two messuages, cottages or dwelling houses situate in Grassington at or near Scaw Ghyll with the croft or parcel of land adjoining'* [5]

It is not clear what happened at the auction but any potential sale appears to have been vetoed by a petition in the High Court of Chancery by other branches of the Birkbeck family. Having resolved this dispute the building was sold in 1857 for £88 to a Mr William Rogers, otherwise referred to as Rogers of Mafeking, for use as a butter factory.

In 1874 Rogers was succeeded in title by his widow and she it seems was the person who built the barn sometime thereafter. The earlier challenge to the Vernacular Buildings Group's assumption that the eastern part of the property had always been the industrial portion and mill is thus dispelled. The 1852 Ordnance Survey Map clearly showed that this part of the building did not exist at that date. However, the will of Jane Rogers confirmed that the extension was definitely in being by 1893. Susan Brooks stated that: *'She devised the dwelling house wherein she then resided (Scaw Ghyll), being the dwelling house comprised in the last abstracted indenture with stable, barn and close of land to her son Edmund in fee simple and she devised two cottages at the roadside in Grassington in trust for her daughter Amanda.'* [6]

(There were several references at different times to two cottages; it is not clear whether these formed part of Scaw Ghyll or were totally unrelated.) Further corroboration of the dating of the barn was found in a 1916 conveyance that referred to *'A stable, barn and butter warehouse at the north-easterly corner of the hereditments'* [7] of the wheel pit and how power entered the building. Susan Brooks wrote: *'There is no doubt about the existence of the wheel pit which was open to view in Scaw Ghyll yard a few years ago'.* [8]

We now revisit the archaeological evidence pointing to the location. There is also a blocked up window in the dining room, formerly part of the barn, which has been conveniently described as the entry point for a drive shaft from the wheel. Sadly, as has been shown, the dating of the building does not support this hypothesis. I am willing to be convinced that butter making was on such a large scale that water powered churns were required, but I have no knowledge of this process elsewhere in the Dales. This pit cannot however have been the wheel pit for the cotton mill, which occupied the cottages in the western half of the building. Having considered the various options there are three possible explanations:

• The southwest end wall of the cottages could have had a wheel attached. There is certainly space and also a 'pit' which now houses a flight of stairs down to an external cellar entrance. Weaknesses in this argument are that the doorway at the bottom of these stairs appears to be original and it is questionable whether Scaw Ghyll ever had sufficient volume of water to drive a large vertical wheel.

• There could have been a smaller 'barrel-type' wheel somewhere behind the cottages and thus right in the heart of the present building. Such wheels were apparently used where water was limited. This idea is supported by the 1852 map, which shows the stream flowing right under the centre of the building. This seems to fit with the Scaw Ghyll requirement, and a similar wheel can still be seen on a mill in Settle. The stream has been subjected to diverting and culverting further upstream, and so the amount of water originally available is a matter of conjecture, but the map suggests this was always a minor stream. The weakness of this option is that the stream would have had to be diverted very deep underground to flow under the cellars. Again, even a small 'barrel-type' wheel may have been too large and too late in design for the modest mill under consideration.

• The stream may have actually flowed through the cellars to drive a horizontal 'Norse Mill', powering machinery at ground floor level. This would also explain why such substantial cellars were necessary.

It could also be the origin of the open culvert around the back of the house; such a mill could have had a balancing tank and sluice to regulate water flow through or round the property.

'Conclusion' is too strong a word for a building which contains so many secrets. However, having discounted so many previously expressed ideas, I put forward some alternative suggestions:

The original building comprised three units, each approximately 16 feet by 9 feet, and included a barrel vaulted cellar, a ground floor room and a first floor room. All four external walls and one internal partition are 600 mm thick. The second internal partition is also substantial but significantly thinner, 450 mm. My own belief is that the unit nearest the road was always a house whereas the other two units may originally have been the cotton mill. The narrower partition wall could have been added around 1810 when the mill was converted to cottages.

The extensive and substantial cellars support the idea that the building originally had some kind of industrial use. The building is 60 years too old to have been purpose-built as a cotton mill. Taken together these two facts give strong credence to the theory that Scaw Ghyll may originally have been constructed as a corn mill. The idea that this corn mill had its origins as a medieval manorial soke mill is much more speculative. The building was certainly used as some kind of butter warehouse or butter manufacturing plant and it was extended for this purpose by the addition of a barn and stable at the rear of the building in the late 19th century. It is possible that there was a water wheel associated with this butter manufacturing process, but it seems unlikely. Claims that evidence of a wheel pit can be found in the rear yard are improbable. They seem to result from misinterpreting the building as being cottages in the western portion, and a mill on the eastern side.

The original cotton mill and possibly an earlier corn mill must have harnessed the water source, and so Scaw Ghyll must have had a wheel, but all remaining traces of this had disappeared by about 1875. I have considered the various options for the location of this wheel. Based on the date and size of the original mill, the likely volume of water available and required, and the sloping topography of the site, my own hypothesis is that there may have been a small horizontal Norse mill housed in the cellars.

References

1 Report of Upper Wharfedale Field Society Vernacular Buildings Group (No. 1562, 1997).

2 First Edition Ordnance Survey Map 1852.

3 Ingle, George (1997) Yorkshire Cotton, The Yorkshire Cotton Industry 1780-1835, Carnegie Publishing.

4 Title Deeds to Scaw Ghyll (1916 conveyance).

5 Unpublished research papers of Miss Susan Brooks, held at Skipton Reference Library.

6 ibid.

7 Title Deeds.

8 Brooks, Susan.

18. The Common Stream
Grassington's Public Water Supplies

Richard Harland

Water supplies from sources local to the consumer have always given way to more abundant supplies of better quality from sources further afield. The following is an account of the days when Grassington could find sources, though increasingly inadequate, mainly within its own township boundaries.

In most villages former public watering places can be identified. [1] At these, clothes were washed and domestic supplies were carried from a spring, a stream or a trough which might be fed by a pump or by gravity. Grassington had all three. A stream of water, gathered naturally and also by dug conduits, passes through Grassington from the hillside below Spring House and from fields above and below Edge Lane. This

Fig. 38. Grassington Square in the 1920s,
Carrie Gledhill

supply contributed much to the growth of the settlement. It descends, partly ditched, to the head of the old village.

As it runs through streets and public spaces it has been culverted through a rectangular dry-stonewalled channel, roofed with stone flags. Where there is access allowing measurements to be made, the channel's height is almost two feet. The stream crosses from the Main Street, goes through Lucy Fold to the eastern side of the square, and from here, soon after 1850, a feed pipe was run to supply a new facility of troughs fed by a 'fountain' or jet of stream water in the market place – today's 'Square'.

These amenities were the gift of Stephen Eddy (1800-1861), mineral agent to the Duke of Devonshire. Eddy's home, now Grassington House Hotel, overlooked the square, Fig. 39) but by 1859 he had moved to the newly built 'Elbolton' beside the road to Hebden. Maybe there were three troughs, of which today's non-matching sandstone pair, now located further down the Square, survive. They were not brand new from the quarry, for they differ in size and in the nature of the stone.

106

The final lift of water into the troughs was given by a hand-pump housed in the foundry-cast casing with its finial that has become almost an emblem of Grassington. The two iron bands around it were added later for strength, the most recent one in the 1970s. [2] The fountain then stood higher up the Square, but the head of water yielded a good flow from the spout. This fed today's sandstone trough, where a pail could stand on iron straps to be filled; in 1921 at least one resident still relied on it for her home supply. For washing clothes, water could be bucketed to the larger gritstone trough.

Two other watering places are shown on the OS 25-inch plan of 1909. (Except for minor changes, this plan is a record of things as they were in 1890). One is a rough-hewn gritstone trough at the foot of Moor Lane, then known as Yarnbury Road.

Fig. 39. Grassington House,
home of Stephen Eddy
(Edmund Bogg. A 1000 Miles in Wharfedale)

This trough was removed for safety during building work in 1997-2000, and was reinstated almost in the same place, near the side door of the Devonshire Institute. The other trough is at Well Head, outside Craven Cottage on Main Street (Fig. 40).

This was a civic amenity designed with attention to detail, and it remains intact. Its well-crafted twin five-foot sandstone troughs were provided with a stone-flagged apron for users' convenience; this can be seen when parked cars allow. Nearby springs behind the Institute (not water from the stream) are said to have supplied these troughs. All five troughs and the pump were maintained by the parish officers and from 1895 by the parish council, until 1937 when works 'for the gratuitous supply of water to the inhabitants' became vested in Skipton Rural District Council. [3]

The copiously flowing Brow Well near Low Mill was used as a standby in times of drought. Lady Well beside the river in Threshfield was used both in drought and when the service pipes froze in 1940. [Fn1]

Dating evidence for field supplies for the animals is scanty though the Grassington Inclosure Award of 1792 details the liberty granted for owners and occupiers

Fn1. At the period of its supplying Grassington the water collected in a stone trough that is now submerged. A roadside stile giving access to a tiny strip of common land that reaches down to Lady Well enables it to be visited still.

generally and for certain owners specifically, to dig cuts or grips for leading water to their new allotments of land. [4]

These grips would normally terminate at troughs. A few houses had always enjoyed their own private supply from a spring, a well or a rainwater tank. In Grassington, a unique example is the rainwater trough ingeniously contrived in the cottage

Fig. 40. Grassington Town Hall and Well Head
Troughs.
(Carrie Gledhill)

kitchen now forming the rear part of the Grassington museum. After depositing any leaves and litter, the water flowed by lead pipe into the capacious stone cistern of well-dressed stone that we see today. This would have held about 90 gallons.

The next step of progress, available to those who could afford it, was a water supply taken by pipes into private homes. Such schemes were carried out in Settle as early as 1769, in Skipton in 1823 and in Rylstone in about 1830.

Cast-iron pipes were superseding wooden pipes by the end of the 18th century, and manufacturing advances greatly encouraged their use after about 1820. They rendered it practicable to tap a better source even if more distant, and to convey the water without contamination. The supply in Settle was achieved by one resident's enterprise. In Rylstone an individual owning a number of the houses took the initiative.

In Skipton it was a group of local people on the community's behalf who pushed a scheme forward, and in many villages this was the likely option.

It occurred, for example, in Settle in 1843 when the 1769 scheme no longer met the demand, in Embsay in 1854, in Crosshills in 1856 and at Sutton Mill in 1861. Ultimately it occurred in Grassington. A constant supply terminating at Grassington Old Hall was brought in a skilfully engineered 700-yard culvert from a field near the head of Intake Lane. The writer has examined the structure of this culvert from within an inspection chamber that lies under a heavy stone flag in the lane. Before reaching Chapel Street two branches split off, each supplying tanks and troughs in private land, and the main culvert supplied others before reaching its terminus. Whether these intermediate supplies served as wayleave compensation, [Fn1] or whether the landowners had shared in the expense is now impossible to say.

It was described by a local observer as 'A stone culvert like a land drain'. [5] This system of supply is known as Calvert Water. There were Calverts in the parish from the late 17th century, but as it was only in the early 20th century that Calverts appear to have owned the Old Hall; the name may come from the engineer or the contractor involved, or from 19th century ownership of the land from which the water derives. There was also a local plumber named Richard Calvert at that time. [Fn2]

Grassington waited until 1869 for the community to bestir itself to the extent of agreeing upon the need and upon the remedy. On 20 August 1869 a public meeting was convened. With a population that had grown faster than that of any other Wharfedale township, it is remarkable that Grassington had so long endured without radical enhancement of its traditional supply. The meeting acknowledged that the inhabitants of the village 'have hitherto been supplied with a very insufficient quantity of water for their domestic use and other necessary purposes'.

A committee of nine local men was appointed 'for the purpose of procuring a good supply of better water for the inhabitants':, William Wrathall, 42, farmer, Joseph Pattinson, 48, farmer, Thomas Airey, 52, coach proprietor, Mason Lee Fleming, 23, cabinet maker, Robert Pickles, 68, farmer, Thomas B Lee, 49, lead ore dresser, Joseph Robinson, 41, grocer and draper, Thomas Trevethan, 35, lead mine agent and assayer, and William Hartley, 60, innkeeper. [6] Apart from the absence of women, the range of occupations and age in this public-spirited group is impressive.

Five of the nine had been born in the parish. Agreement was provisionally reached with the landowners, and a draft Deed of Arrangement was drawn up. We know only that this was in the 1870s. The committee were to provide field troughs and watering places in compensation for the water led away, and no charge was to be made for supplying them. Details were to be shown on a plan.

The committee concluded that the best sources for the purpose were *'certain springs and streams which arise in or run through lands belonging to Thomas Rathmell, Edward Armstrong and three others named, and disappear after entering the village'* [7] The water was to be collected in a tank and piped down Yarnbury Road. On the evidence of land ownerships, these are in fact the sources used later, after 1887, by the water company.

Fn1. Wayleave compensation is paid for a right of way granted by a landowner, in this case to permit water to cross land by means of a culvert.

Fn2. To find any written reference to Calvert Water, such as in a property Deed, is a challenge for the future. A sketch plan, reconstructing the run of the Calvert Water culvert, was drawn in the 1980s by Don Wilcox. From oral statements he dated the system c.1870. A copy of the plan has been placed in the Grassington Museum. So far as practicable the writer has verified it with help from Sam Pattinson and Susan Dean, and by re-locating one of the Intake Lane inspection chambers.

However, there is no evidence that the Deed was executed, no plan is known to survive, and above all we do not know of action being taken for a further 18 years, except what we can infer as the preparatory arrangements for establishing a water company.

A decisive milestone was the registration on 8 November 1887 of the Memorandum and Articles of Association of the Grassington Water Works Company Ltd, with the objective of supplying the township and adjacent places.

The fourteen shareholders, comprising only two members of the original 1869 committee, were a good mix: two builders, two plumbers, three farmers, a grocer, two grocers and drapers, an innkeeper, a landowner, a 'gentleman' and a manufacturer. The part-time secretary was William Harker, a local government officer of ability.

With landowners' consent, the Company laid pipes from a spring in Edge Top Quarry, which was parish property, running first for a few yards along Edge Lane, and then downhill to a settling tank in Ling-House Pasture, known as Lingass or Lingasses, the two top roadside-fields below Edge Lane.

These, together with the fields Edge Side, next below the two Lingasses, and Edge Top above Edge Lane, were by now owned by James Ray Eddy, who had acquired part in 1880 from Edward Armstrong's executors and the remainder in 1887 after Thomas Rathmell's death. Eddy allowed facilities for the Company to construct various waterworks, among them the rectangular service reservoir in Edge Side which still stands. This was a major advance, for storage enabled a substantial demand to be met from a source yielding even a modest flow, provided it was constant. Alongside the construction of these headworks, the Company laid its distribution system comprising a 4-inch feeder pipe down to the top Square and thence 3-inch and 2-inch mains. Householders would incur the cost of service pipes and inside plumbing, and the disruption.

On 17 May 1889 the Company signalled its readiness to commence supply, by issuing Rates, Rules and Regulations. Not every householder elected at once for a piped supply. Mrs Dorothy Cox, born about 1896, recalled water from the Well Head troughs being fetched by other children for use at home. [8] However, by the start of the new century, the supply was quite insufficient to meet growing demands. One need only recall the residential and tourist influx, and the coming of the railway. There were prolonged discussions. In 1902 terms were almost agreed with Mr Eddy for legally regularising the works already carried out on his land. In 1906 it was resolved to ask him to meet the Directors about obtaining in Lingass *'a further additional supply which is very much needed'*. The 1912 AGM of the Company discussed a motion on *'the best method of raising money to meet the cost of an increased Water Supply which is urgently needed and to give sanction to such a scheme and the cost thereof'*. [9]

In 1913 a 120-foot well was sunk in Lingass with Mr Eddy's consent. The company's capital was raised from £1000 to £1500. Despite the facilities provided by Mr Eddy in Edge Side and Lingass, the company was convinced that more could be done to augment the supply if those fields, together with land above Edge Lane, were owned freehold.

Towards the end of 1913 negotiations were in hand. Then the War intervened. Only after Eddy's death in 1919 did it become practicable to acquire from his executors the land then seen to be needed: Edge Side and the two Lingasses below Edge Lane, and Edge Top above it, amounting to almost 41 acres. To finance the consequent works as well as the laying of new distribution mains, the authorised capital was raised to £2500 in that year. Trading was profitable and the mortgage on the land was paid off in 1927.

Following the Company's land acquisition, a 78-foot borehole was sunk in Edge Top and four springs were harnessed. In 1937 the storage was more than doubled by building a new circular reservoir in Edge Side, close to the existing rectangular one.

In 1939, at the outbreak of World War II, there was an influx of troops and evacuees. The War Department recognised that more water would be needed, so a ram-pump was installed at Brow Well, and until 1942 water was fed into the system through the mains in Hebden Road. Even so, the village supply was frequently shut off from 10 pm to 7.45 am, probably because of a need to minimise loss through leakage from the pipes. From 1944 routine chlorination of the water supply enabled alternative sources to be utilised, but in an emergency, non-chlorinated water from Lady Well and from Brow Well was fed into the mains using fire service hoses and pumps.

Despite its problems the company provided a good network of mains water supply throughout the village. A map, probably representing what was in place by 1949, shows a well-planned and compact water undertaking with sources, adits, two service reservoirs, and distribution mains with some major service pipes. Demand and maintenance costs were constantly increasing and it was common to find that local water undertakings, through charging a low water rate, accumulated insufficient funds for maintenance and improvement.

When heavy spending was needed, the company sought to transfer responsibility, so in 1945 the Parish Meeting, in desperation, asked Skipton Rural District Council to take over the supply, which was done on April 1st, 1949. The council carried this responsibility for ten years, its most striking achievement being to supplement the supply by piping water from the adjoining township of Hebden. In 1959 Skipton joined with five other councils in establishing the Craven Water Board so that supplies could be coordinated over a wider area.

We must now look beyond the township. When the sanatorium in Hebden Road was opened in 1919, the works included a substantial tank at the top of its grounds, adjoining Edge Lane. The water came no great distance from a source near Garnshaw. This soon proved insufficient, and in about 1924 pipes and a pumphouse were installed for feeding into the tank, from a distance of more than a mile. The water flowed out of the Duke's Level, a lead mine drainage adit driven under Grassington Moor to Hebden Gill between 1780 and 1825.

In 1958 the Council agreed terms with the hospital authority for augmenting the Grassington supply from its tank, and almost 1400 yards of pipes were laid to the reservoirs in Edge Side. However the water from Duke's Level proved to be at risk of pollution from the many mineshafts on the moor, and despite chlorination this was not acceptable. It fell to the Craven Water Board to deal with the problem.

This was done in 1963 by a complex scheme, again in Hebden Gill, for harnessing a stream of water issuing from the rock near the head of a much shorter and more controllable lead mine adit known as Lanshaw Level. This water passed all tests for purity, but as a further safeguard, the few mine shafts that might indirectly communicate with the Level were fenced around. The freeholders of Hebden, as owners of the mineral rights, were paid compensation for the loss of mineral royalties proportionate to their 'ancient rents'. [10]

Abstraction of water had to be moderated to avoid depleting the beck below a minimum flow set by the Rivers Authority, for which purpose a flow-gauge was built close above Hole Bottom Bridge. The hospital's pipeline, pumphouse and tank were acquired and most of those in Hebden Gill were abandoned. A holding tank was built outside the mouth of the level and a pipe was laid to a new chlorination and pump house at Hole Bottom. The Duke's Level supply could now be abandoned, save as an emergency standby for the hospital and for Grassington and on account of that potential use, the portal to the Level was blocked to prevent unauthorised entry.

The scheme gave relief to Grassington's own sources by restricting the demand upon them to that of the upper village. Below a valve in Main Street, water now came from Lanshaw Level, through the chlorination plant at Hole Bottom into the sanatorium tank, and by a new pipeline across the Wharfe below the church stepping stones (incidentally setting the route of the river crossing for ICI's Teesside to Runcorn ethylene pipeline). This new main now supplied Linton and Thresh field, so the public water trough outside the cottages at Botany in Church Road fell out of domestic use, and the lower part of Grassington village was fed through existing mains near the bridge.

The tale has now reached the stage defined in the opening words: to meet any further demands for water, Grassington now needed substantially to be supplied from sources outside the township boundaries. Subsequent changes therefore lie outside the scope of this account.

Sources:

Other information derives from the writer's notes and memory, and from files and property deeds transferred to Craven Water Board by Skipton Rural District Council in 1959. The Board's archives were listed by Miss Murdoch of the National Register of Archives, the task being completed in May 1965 under their ref. C193; the writer has given a copy to the County Library, Skipton Branch. The Grassington documents form item 562. In 1974 the files and deeds were transferred (along with the writer) to Yorkshire Water Authority. In 1988 (without the writer) the deeds were doubtless transferred to Yorkshire Water Company but it is not known whether the files have survived. Since no other source seems available for some of the information it has seemed helpful to recount the story here.

See also Appendix D.

References

1 Hartley, Marie and Ingleby, Joan (1990) Life and Tradition in the Moorlands of North-East Yorkshire, Otley: Smith Settle pp.43 and 101.

2 Harland, Richard (1961) Oral History of the Culvert, Trough and Pump in the 'square', Craven Herald, Skipton 18/11/61.

3 The parish council was established by the Local Government Act 1894. Public watering places went over to the District Council under the Public Health Act 1936

4 Certain field supplies of the late 18th century are identifiable from Henry Waddington and Thomas Ingilby (Commissioners): Award upon the Inclosure of the several stinted pastures called Old Pasture, New Pasture, Botton and Lossgill-Bank in the township of Grassington (1792, reprinted at The Pioneer Office, Skipton, 1874), pp 37-8.

5 Hartley and Ingleby (1990).

6 The work of the Craven Water Board during its 15-year life is recorded in its Report on the Work of the Board 1959-1974 (1974). On p.11 the Hebden Gill scheme is listed, on p.24 is a photograph of the Crump Weir (the flow gauge) in Hebden Beck, and on p.9 the two necessary statutory orders are named. A copy of the Report is in the County Library, Skipton branch.

7 ibid.

8 Mrs Dorothy Cox's memories were collected by Helen Lefevre on 12th April 1990; the writer has given her note to Grassington Museum.

9 ibid. Harland

10 Joy, David (1991) Uphill to Paradise, Skipton: Jerry & Ben's, private publication, p.40.

19. Alternating Currents –
An Electrical Undertaking

Herbert Masterson

Large electricity supply undertakings in Britain, both municipal and public, attracted brisk investment in the early years of the twentieth century. Their history is well charted in contemporary publications, which have been a fruitful source of research material. Public companies set up in small communities to provide a local electric light supply have had less attention. Their relative neglect is understandable. Individually, they were less newsworthy, and, as a group, they played only a minor role in rural electrification. In the Yorkshire Dales, as elsewhere, most early village lighting schemes were provided by mill or landowners as a secondary activity, usually with no separate commercial identity.

There are many examples. The Gill family of New York mill in Summerbridge gave Nidderdale its first electric light on a limited scale in 1891, benefiting the chapel and a few houses. Further up that dale at Pateley Bridge, it was estimated in 1900 that investment of £2,000 would enable the surplus power at Mr Wood's corn mill to supply 750 lamps, and by 1903, two companies had applied to the District Council for permission to lay mains in the township. When Mr J A Farrer of Ingleborough Hall in Clapham near Settle developed a hydro-electric scheme in 1893 to power his sawmill, he also lit the Hall, the Church, the home farm, his agent's house and the village reading room, and provided thirteen street lights. In Upper Wharfedale, Hartlington sawmill's water wheel provided a supply for a joiner's shop and some consumers in Burnsall. The Institute at Skireholme, adjacent to the village paper mill, had a large billiard room and kitchen lit with electric light, and AC supplies were provided later at both Hebden and Kilnsey. There was also a municipal installation – Bradford Corporation decided in 1911 to provide a dedicated generating facility at its Consumption Sanatorium for Women at Edge Side on the Grassington-Hebden road.

In the first decade and a half of the twentieth century 20 or so small electric light undertakings were recorded in contemporary electrical journals as registered public companies in England. Some seem to have left no record beyond the fact of company registration. Only two small Yorkshire companies are listed, and these are both in Upper Wharfedale.

The Grassington Electric Supply Company Ltd was set up in 1909 after two years spent canvassing support, and even then had secured less than a fifth of its £1,000 initial capitalisation when contracts were signed. By contrast, the Kettlewell Electricity Supply Company Ltd was inaugurated in 1913 with its capitalisation of £650 already paid-up. It enjoyed the support of Mr Ottiwell Robinson JP, a wealthy mill and landowner living in the village, noted for his local benefactions, and it was able to tempt the competent Skipton engineer, John Banks, away from his allegiance to the larger Grassington Company to set up the Kettlewell system.

With a compact distribution area and little need for development, the Kettlewell Company enjoyed business stability. The Grassington Company, with a much larger potential customer catchment area, was tempted into continual expansion which its access to capital could barely support. In origin it was a self-help enterprise by local entrepreneurs determined to improve the amenities of their community. It remained a small business run by directors elected by shareholders. Directors' meetings seldom attracted more than the necessary quorum. General meetings of shareholders also drew small numbers, and often were not representative of shareholdings. Retention of competent staff was difficult and adequate capital provision always elusive. Despite this, the company succeeded in providing a supply to an extending customer base in this Dales community for over a decade. A review of its history offers an opportunity to explore how business was conducted in this type of village enterprise, and how those who managed it responded to the various influences exerted on them.

Employment at the local mill at Linton ended in the middle of the 19th century, and underground lead mining was killed off by cheap imports, mainly from Spain, with which the deep and thin-veined local mines could not compete, by 1877. Between the Census years 1851 and 1891 Grassington's population dropped from 1138 to 480. At the start of the 20th century here was a will to attract tourists and new residents in order to revive the village fortunes. A group of local people formed the Grassington Waterworks Company Ltd in 1887 to renew the village water supply, and a sewerage system was installed.

When the Yorkshire Dales Railway reached the area in July 1902, it brought not only tourists but also several wealthy new residents from Bradford, now within commuting range.

That city's Corporation had installed Britain's first municipal power station in 1889 and its more affluent citizens were already accustomed to electric light in their homes.

Although electric lighting in the early 1900s was confined generally to commercial properties and large private houses in towns, a village project in Grassington could have expected reasonable support.

When John Fielden, a Skipton tailor, bought the unoccupied five storey Linton water mill in 1907 (Fig. 41) (possibly as a speculation influenced by the Lancashire mill building boom of 1904-8), John Crowther, the Grassington chemist and a local worthy, saw an opportunity of basing a village lighting scheme there. His interest came to the notice of a Bradford electrical contractor, Charles Pullan, who recommended the installation of a water turbine and generator on the washout sluice of the upper of Linton mill's two weirs (Fig. 41). Mr Fielden agreed to lease the water rights, and the Grassington Electric Supply Co. Ltd (GESCL) was formed in 1909 to raise capital to implement the scheme. The first directors were Messrs. Crowther and Fielden, with Mr Sam Lee JP as Chairman.

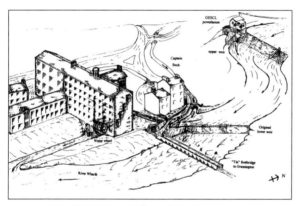

Fig. 41. Linton Mill and the Powerhouse

GESCL's powerhouse at the upper weir was a small wooden building with a corrugated iron roof and a lean-to over the turbine pit. Cables crossed the river to a distribution board at the bottom of the village and current was delivered to consumers at 230v by cables, mainly supported on brackets attached to chimneys.

Major Roundell of Gledstone Hall presided over the official opening, which was marked by a fifty-strong procession and followed by a hotel dinner lit by the new electric light.

The early major investors seemed each to have a personal interest in the company. Mr Fielden already had tenants at the mill and would want to encourage any new rent-paying undertaking on his property. Mr Lowcock, another Skipton tailor, soon to buy Linton mill, would seek, naturally, to have some influence in GESCL, which held water rights to the mill's upper weir. In a different vein, Mr Lee had by his several benefactions evidenced an enduring fondness for his native village, and Mr Elliott, a substantial coal merchant in Bradford, had retired to live there. They had the will to support GESCL, and the coal industry had provided them with the means to do so. Mr Alfred Wall of Pontefract had property investments in the area, and his relatives, the Frielinghaus family, lived in Grassington.

Much of the management of the company in its early years fell to Mr Crowther. He found capital hard to raise, profitability too low to pay dividends, and competent engineers difficult to retain. There was also an expensive dispute with Mr Pullan. Despite this, company income rose acceptably and Grassington Parish Council was persuaded, eventually, to replace its 24 street oil lamps with electric light. However, early in 1911, a special shareholders' meeting was required to address the capital shortfall. Mr Wall, by taking sixty of the unsold shares, gave the others confidence, and Mr Lowcock capped the proceedings by taking the last forty. However, the need for capital soon outstripped the original capitalisation.

By mid-1911, Messrs Crowther, Lowcock, Wall, and Elliott were committed to bonds to the bank totalling £150, and an increase in share capital to £1500 was agreed at the following AGM. Mr Crowther resigned, and Mr Lowcock was elected chairman in his place. About this time, Mr Lowcock bought a half share in Linton mill from Mr Fielden, and formed with him the Linton Mill Estate Co Ltd (LMECL) to manage it. He also formed the Linton Mill Manufacturing Co Ltd with his two sons, Francis and Edward, to run a cotton manufacturing business there.

1912 started brightly for GESCL. Grassington Wesleyan Chapel installed electric light and the GESCL system was extended from Grassington to the adjoining township of Threshfield. The number of lights supplied was twice that of the previous year, and better use of the company's plant outside lighting-up hours was secured by providing increased power supplies. When Mr Lowcock chaired the third AGM, there was satisfaction that revenue had doubled. There would be no dividend that year, but the company had made a good profit, and 'was now on the highway to success'. The 500 new ordinary shares had been taken up quickly, half by Mr Wall alone. However, early in 1912, Linton mill burned down. Although the GESCL plant was unaffected, the fire had a major influence on that company's future. During reconstruction, LMECL replaced the old mill waterwheel with a large water turbine which not only powered a rope drive to the mill main shaft but also ran a generator more than twice as large as GESCL's. In meeting their growing consumer demand, GESCL directors now had the new option of buying a supply from the mill company, rather than finding capital for additional generating plant of their own.

Before the year's end, flood water swept away the centre portion of the upper weir. GESCL lost the use of its in-house generator, and became entirely dependent on the newly-installed LMECL turbine until the weir was repaired in August 1913.

Although income had increased by 20%, the company had made a loss. Even so, the shareholders, many of whom were consumers, encouraged the directors to buy a second-hand oil engine from Wheatleys of Leeds. Perhaps they were influenced by a large bill from LMECL for 'a special extra supply' while the GESCL turbine was out of service, but they were certainly concerned about the priority the Lowcocks had given to the mill's needs at the expense of the village lighting supply.

Discussion at the fifth AGM in 1914 was led by Mr Frielinghaus, Mr Wall's nephew and an electrical engineer. His theme was the adverse cash flow position of the company. The oil engine had turned out to be an expensive option, consumers' meters were not tamper-proof, their inaccuracy was not in the company's favour, and the outstanding capital debt was burdensome. He called for a Special General Meeting to consider advertising the company for sale as a going concern, which implies that Frielinghaus, an electrical engineer, had lost confidence in that prospect by then. This meeting, held in November, was poorly attended, with Mr Frielinghaus a notable absentee, and the resolution failed.

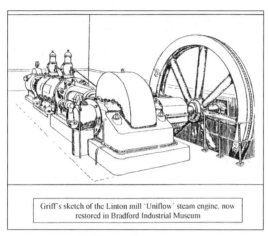

Griff's sketch of the Linton mill 'Uniflow' steam engine, now restored in Bradford Industrial Museum

Fig. 42. The Uniflow Steam Engine

The number of consumers continued to rise satisfactorily in the early war years, but the GESCL system remained unreliable and directors were unable to retain a competent engineer to deal with it. They found themselves increasingly reliant on LMECL supplies. They decided to buy a 14 year-old National suction gas engine from the Bradford firm of Millar, Dennis & Co, whose director, J D Dennis, came to live in Threshfield in 1915. These engines were seen at that time as compact, economical, and normally requiring little attention. Mr Fielden severed his link with the company about this time, selling his shares to Mr A J Plunkett, a coal merchant living in Threshfield, who became the new company chairman.

In November 1917, the company had a further influx of new shareholders who had bought Mr Wall's holding following his death the previous year. Two of these, Mr Dennis and Mr F S Clayton, another Bradford engineer resident in Threshfield, were co-opted to the board at the AGM to strengthen technical discussion. Revenue had dropped, attributed by Mr Plunkett to the absence of a company engineer for the greater part of the year.

By 1918 income had doubled again, but the suction gas engine remained unreliable, and there was further dependence on LMECL electricity during the summer water shortage. The distribution system was deteriorating too, and the directors renewed their efforts to engage a competent electrician.

A major challenge came in 1919 when LMECL, responding to the post-war cotton boom, decided to buy a large steam-driven power plant for the mill (Fig. 42). GESCL directors were asked to commit themselves to a ten-year supply contract, but concluded that 'the company could not enter into a contract to purchase current generated by so large a power-plant as purposed being installed by LMECL owing to the high cost of production compared with this company's requirements'. The GESCL directors still believed the suction gas plant was their cheapest option and decided to get it into full working order.

Mr Dennis arranged for one of his Bradford engineers to examine the plant and to instruct GESCL's new engineer, Mr Musto, how to run it. The directors also decided to look for a second-hand 40 kwW dynamo to supplement the 20 kW dynamo they already had. This positive line soon faded, faced with continuing difficulties with the gas plant. The directors passed the Mitchell Dennis report to Mr Musto, with instructions to 'effect the necessary repairs at once'. Instead, he resigned. They had paid his expense claim for board and lodging only 'under protest', and since they had been considering 'what they deemed to be necessary in the way of heating and accommodation to make the power house comfortable', it may be they expected Mr Musto to live in there with the plant. By 1920, the GESCL directors had returned to the possibility of taking all their electricity requirements from LMECL, but now found the Lowcock terms unacceptable.

The future of GESCL as a separate generating company looked bleak. The directors agreed to follow Mr Lowcock's proposal to canvass shareholders to support a proposal to sell the company.

Although the company's income had increased yet again by 20%, the main business of the tenth AGM was a review by Mr Plunkett of a meeting which directors had held with consumers at Grassington Town Hall. The consumers had been briefed on the difficulties the company faced in continuing to supply electricity at a reasonable price and had been asked 'what material support may be relied on in the event of further capital expenditure being necessary' Mr Plunkett reported that the directors 'had received much encouragement and indications of financial support if they would present a thoroughly reliable Electric-Lighting Scheme as soon as possible' and they commissioned Mr B N Dadge of Brighouse to devise one. Although not recorded as present, Mr Crowther was heartened: 'Business people from 'the city' (Bradford, forsooth!) are erecting palatial dwellings, and the struggles of the local electric lighting company are expected soon to be overcome, and develop into a strong corporation...'

However when GESCL directors presented Mr Dadge's report, and its costs, in Grassington Town Hall in July, *the consumers had no alternative to offer to the proposed sale*'.

By the end of 1920, the company had been advertised for sale and two offers received: £375 from LMECL and £550 from a Mr Fisher. The directors accepted the latter. A directors' meeting then heard Mr Lowcock's explanation of a difficulty which had arisen between Mr Fisher and LMECL over the security of tenure of the water rights. In the absence of a resolution of this problem, the meeting adopted a proposal to put the company into voluntary liquidation, on the grounds that the level of its debts made it legally unable to continue in business. Having decided on this course, the directors then accepted an offer by LMECL, matching that of Mr Fisher, to buy the company. The liquidation proposal was endorsed at an EGM in January 1921, the company secretary, Mr G J Harker, being appointed liquidator.

The Gazette announced the last General Meeting of the company to be held at the Wilson Arms, Threshfield, on the 17th June 1924. Mr Harker reported receipts of £1007 14s. 4d. and payments of £988 19s. 4d. With the balance of £18 15s., the company declared its one and only payment of 3d. in the £ on its paid up capital of £1500.

Available data on GESCL's performance is sparse but some analysis is possible. Until 1912, the company seems to have made steady progress, despite the cost of the Pullan dispute. It was selling most if not all of its production capacity (61% committed by autumn 1910) and its income was sufficient to allow reduction of its initial debt. Lack of capital from sale of shares was the main problem. John Crowther deplored the lack of support from property owners and the Parish Council in those early years. However, two of the local gentry, Sir Matthew Wilson and Major Roundell (his son-in-law) did take shares. Their interest may well have been to support Major Roundell's political career, but Sir Matthew, in particular, had widespread investment interests and would have expected GESCL to provide a reasonable return. Good electricity companies offered about 5% p.a. at that time, with the prospect of additional bonuses.

He sent his agent, Mr J W Broughton, to the Shareholders' meeting in 1910, and attended the 1914 meeting in person, but was not convinced, apparently, that further investment would be worthwhile. The Parish Council's reluctance to invest, on the other hand, may have reflected the view of the Dales farmers, who were chided in the local press for their opposition to the use of the parish rates to benefit Grassington dwellers.

Access to the substantial generating capacity at Linton mill enabled the directors to extend their distribution system, and thereby increase their income from consumers. However, consumer dissatisfaction with the quality of supply also pushed them to capital expenditure in old second-hand generating equipment requiring maintenance beyond the level of engineering competence they were prepared to employ. The wave of new shareholders, represented by Mr Plunkett's purchase of Mr Fielden's shares in 1915, and by the group of investors, mainly business people from Bradford, and mostly GESCL consumers, who split Mr Wall's large holding equally between them in 1917, seems to have reinforced the trend towards consumer orientation in company direction. Their purchase of shares did not increase GESCL's capitalisation, but they supported GESCL's provision of additional plant and favoured the Dadge plan to augment GESCL's water generation capacity. This would have impinged further on efficient water-power management at the mill, and although Mr Plunkett failed to persuade his fellow shareholders to fund it, the move may have influenced the Lowcocks to consider it was time to buy GESCL out. They had the capital and the engineering resources at the mill to make electricity supply the profitable symbiotic enterprise which fellow mill owners had found it to be. Acquiring GESCL would also gain them operational control of the mill site and water supply, which Mr Fielden had let go. It was a commercial opportunity which the Lowcocks were well placed to evaluate and to take.

How did that opportunity come about? One possibility is that there was simply an adverse cash flow unrelieved by corrective management action, perhaps through failure to impose a limit on growth of consumer demand and increase charges sufficiently to fund the enterprise fully.

With reservations over the data, particularly for annual expenditure, the vulnerability of GESCL's trading position in its last few years of operation was not obvious. Nor could the main problem have been funding long-term debt. Interest payment on the outstanding bank mortgage of only £400 would have placed little strain on the company. The weight of LMECL charges were rising with growing consumer demand as GESCL acted increasingly as LMECL's agent.

The impact of this burden seems tolerable too, although subject to the Lowcock's future charging policy. However, the liquidator's report offers further insights. LMECL was owed an additional £146, and was, in fact, the only creditor in a position to threaten liquidation. The report also highlights the trading weakness which left the company vulnerable to this threat. Income was lagging expenditure heavily. While GESCL's debts were more than covered by income due to it, the outstanding debt due from consumers at liquidation stood at over £400, and of this, a quarter was owed by directors and shareholders, past or present. The GESCL Board was reluctant, apparently, to press its fellows for prompt payment, even at this juncture. Certainly, shareholders' long term view was discouraging. No dividend had been paid since inauguration, none was now likely, and recovery of invested capital was doubtful. In this small close community, a perception that payment of electricity bills might prudently be avoided, or at least long delayed, might have spread rapidly. It may well be that it was this inability to collect consumer charges, joined with LMECL's concern that recovery of its growing debt was becoming precarious, which triggered the liquidation decision.

However it came about, the absorption of the GESCL undertaking into the Lowcock family business led to a step change. Hydro-generation capacity was increased both at the upper weir and at the mill, and the distribution system was mostly re-built. This required a much-needed capital injection of about £14,000, but income from the regenerated business, which doubled to £1,000 in the year following take-over, more than doubled again the following year, and the Lowcock family companies continued to provide the electricity supply of the area until nationalisation brought connection to the national grid.

Acknowledgements

Masterton, Herbert (1999) An Electrical Undertaking in Upper Wharfedale in the Early 1900's. The Yorkshire Archaeological Journal Vol. 71.

The Yorkshire Archaeological Society for kind permission to reprint a condensed version of the original article.

West Yorkshire Archive Service.

Reference Librarians of Skipton, Bradford, and Preston Libraries.

Peter Fethney, Curator of Grassington Museum, for permission to use the minutes of the Grassington Electric Supply Co. Ltd.

Griff Hollingshead, for his encouragement and for altering his drawing to provide Fig. 42.

Jack Dobson, for permission to use his notebook, which belonged formerly to Mr Harry Moss.

Turbine and Generating House
From John Crowthers 'Rambles Around Grassington', 1920

Memories from Craven

20. The Total Eclipse 1927
Craven Memories

Richard Harland

The eclipse occurred at about half past six on the midsummer morning of 29th June, at which time viewers saw the moon cover the sun. Complete totality was predicted on the centre line of a band 30 miles wide, crossing from Hartlepool, through Darlington and Richmond, to Southport Pier. An estimated fifty thousand people gathered on Richmond racecourse, and a quarter of a million on Southport beach. Where the band crossed Swaledale the AA afterwards erected a roadside plaque. From Brewster Mount Scarborough (now known as the Harland Mount Nature Reserve), though well outside the band, I saw something of it from behind a cloud. Most viewers were well rewarded by a fine clear sky but a few were disappointed; clouds were moving across and mist arose in patches, so even climbing to a hilltop did not guarantee a good sighting.

The sighting of the eclipse in Littondale was obscured by mist for the crucial moments. Litton lay within the band, and so people converged upon it. Janet Taylor, in her book *Littondale Life 1870-1990*, has described how some of these visitors expected to find a village with shops for buying provisions, but instead found themselves dependent on the generous hospitality of residents. Giggleswick was internationally famed as the place to go, its name becoming almost synonymous with the eclipse. It had good rail and road access, and Giggleswick School offered facilities. The Astronomer Royal and others from Greenwich Observatory joined the crowds in a field below the school chapel, where a big telescope was erected and *The Daily Sketch* newspaper organized chairs and camera equipment. The world, as it were, gathered from far and wide, and residents in Sutton, Skipton and Coniston Cold recall an enormous volume of motor traffic travelling throughout the night to Giggleswick. Excursion trains jammed the lines.

A train carrying school children was halted outside Giggleswick station. However, they still enjoyed a splendid view of the eclipse from the carriage windows. Some schools had been granted a half-holiday and mill workers at Cononley were allowed a late start. Some school groups who had travelled to Giggleswick by train spent the rest of the day on walks with their teachers; one group went to Malham Cove, another to Giggleswick Scar.

The late Arthur Gemmell, then a boy from Yeadon School exhilarated by his first sight of Ingleborough, gained a life-long commitment to the hills that day. Many children, woken early by their parents, treasure vivid memories of the whole experience, which was recognized as an historic event. Of course school children were set to write essays on the experience, and two viewers spoke of their childish fear: 'Being a child I was absolutely terrified, didn't know what it was all about' and 'Like most children we thought the world would end that morning'.

Among the journalists present was Arthur Mee, editor of The Children's Newspaper, whose photograph of the blackened sun ringed by prominences of flame was cut out and saved by one six-year old reader who still has it amongst her memorabilia.

Craven folk, ever resourceful, found a variety of viewpoints, including the summit of Buckden Pike, where clouds hid the sun. A student living in Shipley cycled to Starbotton the previous evening, slept briefly in a hayloft, and at 3 a.m. set off up the Pike. There, on the summit, cooking breakfast, he found Arthur Raistrick accompanied by Elizabeth Chapman, his future wife. Indeed, Dr Raistrick himself used to tell of a crowd of viewers gathering, some in the dark, needing to be guided away from the peat bogs. Less far from home, people gathered on Swinden Hill near Cracoe, Park Hill above Skipton, Butter Haw and Mickleber above Gargrave, up Stockard Lane above Cononley and on a hill above Coniston Cold. They perched on wall tops at Greenhow Hill, and even on Rylstone church roof. Some remember how they saw it just as well from their own farm field near Fancarl above Hebden, or from a farm gate at Embsay, a barnyard at Coniston Cold or a doorstep at Draughton Bottom.

Advice had been strongly given to view the sun only through smoked glass, or the goggles of celluloid and card issued free by a newspaper.

A black photograph negative might equally well have been used. Most people remember their smoked glass; many had made their own with candle smoke, or over the fire. The glass could, of course, be put aside with safety during the moment of totality.

There is consistency in the memories of Craven folk who remember watching a huge red sun rising in the sky, shining clear and calm. The moon was seen moving towards the sun, finally sliding closer to obscure it, as the temperature dropped suddenly, and the bright morning went dark and cold. It seemed uncanny and weird: almost everyone recalled how the birds' dawn chorus stilled. One viewer spoke of the consternation of cattle, sheep, and horses who gave mouth to their protest as the darkness grew; another recalled sheep running round as if lost. Hens returned to their roosts and cattle settled down to rest. All nature became calm, deathly quiet, the viewers standing silent. Then came the moment of totality, lasting less than half a minute, when the sun's corona or halo of deep bluish-purple and gold was seen in all its glory, shooting out tongues of flame. The awe-inspiring beauty of those seconds has never been forgotten.

All too soon the moon slipped away and the sun came out, causing a wind. Birds renewed their chorus, hens emerged from their roosts and farm stock resumed grazing. What stays in the memory is the uncanny eeriness of that stillness.

In 1999, the year of our last solar eclipse, the author appealed through the Craven Herald for personal recollections of the 1927 eclipse.

These are the vivid descriptions of the eyewitnesses who responded.

On Long Ridge, Middleton Moor

21. Drawings of Old Grassington

Carrie Gledhill

THOMAS H. GLEDHILL.

Tin, Iron and Copper Plate Worker.

Specialities ⟨ Dairy Utensils, Bins, Etc.
⟨ Repairs of any description.

— Contracts Given for Window Cleaning —

Works : - - Private Address :
Opposite Station. MAIN STREET,
GRASSINGTON.

APARTMENTS.

For comfort and cleanliness (Board optional)

WRITE TO . . .

MRS. GLEDHILLS,

:: *Main Street, Grassington.*

Gledhill family advertisements from
John Crowthers Rambles Around Grassington, 1920

22. Appendices

Appendix A: The Woodd Family of Oughtershaw

A.1: From Arthur Young, (1770) A Farmer's Tour Through the North of England, Vol. 2, London: W. Strahan,

'At Greenfield, in the parish of Arncliffe in Craven, he (Mr. Thos. Elliot of Fremington) has a contiguous tract of 2080 acres of moorland... His design was to inclose and improve a field every year; and this he accordingly has executed annually for several years. The method he takes to improve the black moorland is this: he first pares burns and limes it, then sows it in turnips... The next year he sows turnips again. After this he lays it down to pasture... Potatoes he also cultivates in this black soil... turns out very good profitable pasture... Two acres of it will carry a cow thro' summers well.

Limestone land he manages in same manner; but crops are much greater... Mr Elliot in general lays it down as a maxim, never to attempt any improvements without inclosing: he takes in a field every year... He has improved in a few years 200 acres... Greenfield is a name given to his farm from appearances of green fields in the midst of black deserts.'

A.2: Notes on Paring and Burning for intaking land from moor, transcribed by Richard Harland from notes taken at a lecture by Arthur Raistrick:

1) Pare 4" thick turf with a paring spade, turn upside down and leave a week.

2) Then pile turfs in a heap, around a rolled sod on its end. Heap 3" high and 6" diameter.

3) Burn the heap.

4) Plough in the ash and dress with lime.

5) Sow with turnips, (or cabbages where soil is sandy).

6) Second crop: cabbages.

7) Seed with grass.

A.3: From Arthur Young, (MDCCLXXI), Six Months Tour Through the North of England, Vol. IV, London: Strahan, Nicall, Cadell and Balfour.

<u>POSSIBLE CALCULATION OF THE HORSE POWER OF A 15'-0" DIA.</u>
<u>WATER WHEEL AT GRASSINGTON LOW MILL.</u>

PERIPHERAL SPEED OF WHEEL $\boxed{S = 2\sqrt{R}} = 2 \times \sqrt{7.5} = 5.48$

ie. $S = 5.48$ FT/SEC.

CIRCUMFERENCE OF 15' DIA WHEEL $C = \pi D = 3.14 \times 15$

$\therefore \underline{C_1 = 47.1 \text{ FT}}$

$P = \dfrac{C}{S} = $ SECONDS PER REVOLUTION $= \dfrac{47.1}{5.48} = 8.6$ SECS PER REV.

REVS PER MINUTE R.P.M. $= \dfrac{60 \text{ SECONDS}}{P} = \dfrac{60}{8.6} = \underline{7 \text{ REVS PER MINUTE}}$

HEAD OR FALL OF WATER $\boxed{H = 1.7 R} = 1.7 \times 7.5 = \underline{12.75 \text{ FT.}}$

$C_2 = \underline{\text{ESTIMATED}}$ CIRCUMFERENCE OF WHEEL FULL OF WATER $\boxed{\frac{1}{3} C_1}$

$d = \underline{\text{ESTIMATED}}$ DEPTH OF BUCKET $= 8"$

$\therefore$ WATER IN $\frac{1}{3}$ OF WHEEL $= \dfrac{47.1}{3} \times \dfrac{8"}{12}$ ✱ $\underline{3 \text{ FT. WIDE}} = 31.4$

ie. 31.4 CU. FT OF WATER

1 CU. FT OF WATER $= 62.5$ LBS

$W = $ WEIGHT OF THAT WATER $31.4 \times 62.5 = \underline{1,962.5 \text{ LBS OF WATER}}$

$33,000$ FT. LBS PER MINUTE $= 1$ HORSE POWER

$\therefore$ FOR A $\underline{3' \text{ WIDE}}$ WHEEL $H.P = \dfrac{W \times H \times RPM}{33000} = \dfrac{1962.5 \times 12.75 \times 7}{33000} = \underline{5.3 \text{ H.P}}$

" " $\underline{4' \text{ WIDE}}$ " " $= \dfrac{5.3}{3} \times 4 = \underline{7 \text{ H.P.}}$

" " $\underline{5'-6" \text{ "}}$ " " $= \dfrac{5.3}{3} \times 5.5 = \underline{9.7 \text{ H.P.}}$

FACTORS RINGED $\bigcirc$ ARE
EMPIRICAL RULES AND CAN VARY.

22/3/04

B.2a. Bloom, Les: Possible Calculation of Horse Power of
15' 0" dia. Water Wheel at Grassington

POSSIBLE ARRANGEMENT OF WATER WHEEL AT GRASSINGTON LOW MILL

DATE MEASURED: 17·3·04.   SCALE 1:50

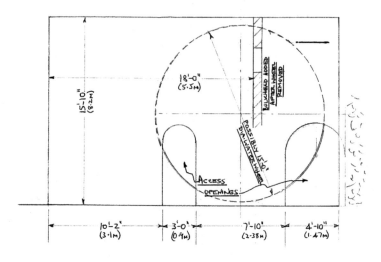

ELEVATION.

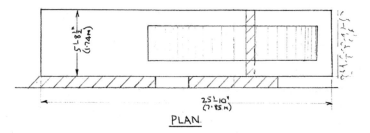

PLAN.

B2b. Possible Arrangement of Water Wheel at Grassington Low Mill   BRONTË BEDFORD-PAYNE & LES. BLOOM.

'*Potatoes he also cultivates in this black soil, in rows two feet asunder, and then sets one foot, and of this he gets often 200 bushels per acre. The grass turns out very good profitable pasture, keeps milch cows, horses, final fattening beasts, sheep, etc., very well.*

Two acres of it will carry a cow through summer well, Some of these grass enclosures are five years old, and rather improve than decay, being better nowe than at first after laying. Some pieces of this lack land which he has enclosed wanted draining, and he has drained such efficiently by drains two feet and a half wide at the top, two feet and half deep, and one foot wide at the bottom. The black earth thrown out he mixes with lime and finds it excellent compost, which answers greatly. Improved worth to a tenant £1-6-0 an acre. Improved would let easily for 8/- an acre.

Appendix B: Corn to Textiles

B.1a. The historical sequence of events at Low Mill between 1597 and 1776 were collated by Susan Brookes of Threshfield, whose studies of papers lodged in the archives of The Yorkshire Archaeological Society in Leeds, the Borthwick Institute in York and the Registry of Deeds in Wakefield led her to publish three booklets, *The Parish and People of Linton in Craven (1967), Parish and People in the Yorkshire Dales Through Ten Centuries (1973),* and *A History of Grassington (1979).* She did not publish all her findings for Grassington Low Mill, but gave her notes to the new owners in 1975. It is from these notes that the early part of the account 'Corn to Textiles at Low Mill' has been written. B2a. and b. Les Bloom Calculations and Drawings.

Appendix C: Friends In Truth

The Quaker Collection at Leeds University's Brotherton Library (Special Collections) ("BL") holds MSS listed in an *Inventory of the Records of Brighouse, Knaresborough, Leeds and Settle Monthly Meetings of the Society of Friends,* Leeds University Library, 2nd. edition, 1997. They include MM minute books from 1666. Local meetings too kept minutes of their meetings for church affairs, and many minute books survive, but not Scarhouse's.

From about 1660 the Quaker structure comprised a national Yearly Meeting, regional Quarterly Meetings (QMs) of which Yorkshire QM was one, a number of Monthly Meetings (MMs) – Settle MM, and Particular Meetings one of which was Scarhouse. This latter was where full gatherings and decision-making meetings took place. All Friends were free to attend MM and QM but only the appointed representatives are recorded in the minutes.

Scarhouse particular meeting, typically of the Dales, embraced a number of townships each with its villages or hamlets. The practice was to meet for Sunday and maybe mid-week worship in 'township groups'. The cited letter of 1654 about a township group in Littondale was from Thomas Taylor and is in Friends House Library, ref. MS VOL.351/18. In 1669 QM defined the MM areas of Yorkshire and their local meetings with township groups at Litton, Arncliffe, Scarhouse and Starbotton, and at [West] Burton in Bishopdale: the document showing this is printed in the *Journal of the Friends' Historical Society* ("FHS"), 1905. 32, p.34; also on pp. x-xiii of Jean and Russell Mortimer (ed.):

Leeds Friends' Minute Book 1692 to 1712, Yorkshire Archaeological Society, ("YAS") Record Series CXXXIX, 1980.

See too BL bundle D9 (record of sufferings 1654-93) for prosecutions in c.1663 for attending township groups at Buckden and Cray: this shows that five or more worshippers met, since that number constituted the crime. Much later, in 1743, Archbishop Herring received reports of township groups in the parishes of Arncliffe (20 attending) and Kettlewell (8 attending) and in Hubberholme chapelry ('about a dozen' attending) [the actual places would be Hawkswick, Starbotton and Deepdale respectively]: *Archbishop Herring's Visitation* Returns 1743 in YAS Record Series LXXII.

Some of the intolerance shown to Friends (their "sufferings") is recorded for Yorkshire in BL bundle D9, and in Joseph Besse: *A Collection of the Sufferings of the People called Quakers 1652 to 1690*, 1753. A facsimile of the Yorkshire section is Besse: *The Yorkshire Sufferings of Early Quakers in Yorkshire 1652 to 1690*, Sessions Book Trust, 1998.

James Tennant farmed under a lease of 1650 from the Earl of Cumberland and of Cork; I dissent from the view (e.g. of Hodgson, *infra*) that this lease was limited to the burial ground plot. BL bundle U23 recites the terms of the lease. Cf. Yorkshire Archaeological Society ref. DD 121

(Skipton Castle papers bundle *25 Rentals in Craven 1640-1700*, and DD 121 Add. Rentals in Craven 1661. Some believe young James Tennant the husband of Ann was grandson to that James but I see him as their son.

Young James' deed of 1709 donating the burial ground says it was his father who acquired the 1650 lease. See also Jane Tennant: *"A brief sketch of the Tennant family from 1500"* (typescript, 1947), in Friends House Library.

For the burial ground see H. R. Hodgson: *The Society of Friends in Bradford*, Bradford, 1926, 74-6. Arthur Raistrick's feeling for the place, and his memories of 1920s working parties to maintain it, are recorded in Bulletin of the Upper Wharfedale Field Society, no.16 (1995), 16. "JT" of the gravestone might be James Tennant who married Elizabeth Rathmell of Linton in 1635 and died in 1674.

George Fox's own account of his 1652 visit to Scarhouse is in the Spence MS which he dictated in Worcester gaol in 1675 and at Swarthmore Hall after release, now printed as Norman Penney (ed.): *The Journal of George Fox, 1911*. I modernise his amanuensis' spelling while keeping his spoken words. The Everyman's Library edition (ed. N. Penney) of 1924 and the 'Cambridge' edition (ed. John L. Nickalls) of 1952 follow the polished literary version compiled after his death and published in 1694.

In 1704 Settle MM at a meeting attended by James Tennant approved a draft statement of what was remembered of the days from spring 1652 to his father's death. This broadly tallies with *The Journal* account; and goes on to say that his father's days of life were *"not Long after ye time of his convincement, being taken Prisoner for his Testimony against Tythes, from which he did not decline, but patiently Endured close imprisonment untill Death"*. This statement was sent to the Quaker office in London and is printed verbatim (except by correcting "takeing" to "taken") in N. Penney (ed.), *The First Publishers of Truth*, FHS, 1907.

The Journal having ended when dictated in 1675, the evidence for his 1677 visit is his letter written from York quoted in David S. Hall: *Richard Robinson of Countersett and the Quakers of Wenslydale,* The Ebor Press, 1989,11, and Edward Haistwell's diary in N. Penney (ed.), *The Short Journal and Itinerary Journals of George Fox,* 1925, 226. In the diary quotation I expand most contractions.

The architectural history of Scarhouse is studied by Kathryn Baird: *The Vernacular Architecture of Buckden and Langstrothdale,* typed M.A. dissertation in the Architecture Library, University of Manchester. As the meeting room Kathryn Baird postulates the downstairs parlour (supposing it to have incorporated the now partitioned-off store). In truth, men and women meeting separately for church affairs would need two rooms, this one as well as the upstairs room where I see them all gathering for worship.

To travel to MM by trap or gig was not an option because the routes were unfit. As late as the 1830s in Arncliffe parish (Langstrothdale and Littondale) *"intercourse even with their nearest neighbours was very exceptional; no one except the farmer moved about, and he chiefly to Skipton or Long Preston fairs on horseback. Indeed sixty years ago [in the 1830s] there was only one single gig in the parish":* Archdeacon Boyd: Fifty Years in Arncliffe being Part I of Littondale Past and Present, 1893.

Quakers must have seemed gadabouts. However circumscribed their outlook, they were not ignorant of the Quaker world beyond the Dale.

Appendix D: The Common Stream

In Dixon, JH (1803-76) *Chronicles and Stories of the Craven Dales, London:* Simpkin, Marshall & Co, the posthumous preface states that the major part of the book was published periodically in 1853-7, so Dr Dixon's information on this matter may be considered contemporaneous with the erection of the fountain. He, with Crowther (below), thought the fountain "exceedingly ugly" and wanted it replaced.

At the 1841 census Stephen Eddy and his wife Sarah resided in the square; by 1851 they had built themselves the house known as Elbolton.

Stephen Eddy's gravestone giving his dates stands in Carleton churchyard: the writer thanks Michael Gill of Sutton in Craven for this information.

Crowther, John (1930), in Silva Gars, Keighley: The Rydal Press repeats Dr Dixon and at pp166-173 inserts his own poem T'owd Pump, dated October 1911, paying tribute both to it and to the donor: *"Thanks to t'good and generous giver/ Who fixed t'owd pump in t'square"* The donor called it a fountain since it ran by gravity with no pumping.

The pump's former location appears in old photographs in Illustrated Guide to Grassington by John Heywood, 1890s and *Higher Wharfedale* by Edmund Bogg, 1904, p242.

A drawing of the pump with its three troughs appears in *Grassington Towards the Millennium* by Ian Goldthorpe, 1999, p9.

A copy of Don Wilcox's sketch plan of the run of Calvert Water 1870, compiled from oral and visual evidence in 1980, can be seen in Grassington Museum.

Roman Stone Pipes found at Grassington
John Crowthers Rambles Around Grassington, 1920

About the Contributors

Heather Beaumont moved to Wharfedale in 1977, after an academic career at the Medical School, University of Birmingham. As warden of Parcevall Hall (The Bradford Diocesan Retreat and Conference House near Appletreewick) she produced booklets on the history of the house and its last private owner, Sir William Milner. She joined the Field Society in the mid 1980s, became a founder member and first leader of its Local History Group in 1989, and served as President of the Society in 1992-3. During this time, she developed an interest in the landscape and documentary history of Barden. In 1992, Heather was a prize-winner in the history essay competition sponsored by the Yorkshire Society. Subsequent publications included a landscape and agricultural history of Barden (Local Historian, 1996) and a year later with Brontë Bedford-Payne, a history of Barden School. In 1994, Heather began a long commitment as joint leader (with David Joy) of the Hebden History Group. As well as a book for general readership, the work of the Group appears in papers dealing with Hebden township boundary, past and present, and the development of the village and agricultural landscape.

Brontë Bedford-Payne studied dentistry at University College Hospital in London, qualifying in 1952, and then practising with her husband in Hertfordshire.

She returned to live in Wharfedale in 1976, when she and her husband established a part-time dental practice in their home, in the newly converted Low Mill, Grassington. For several generations, her mother's family had been tenant farmers in Hanlith, on Malham Moor, and in Barden, on the Duke of Devonshire's Bolton Abbey estate. Early influences included her childhood and schooldays in Barden, where she spent part of the war years. Here, her interest in the ecology and the history of the local landscape was aroused. In 1997 she was joint author, with Heather Beaumont, of 'The Story of Barden School'. She was General Secretary of the Society for seven years before becoming President 1999-2000. She now leads the Local History Group, and is an Honorary Life Member of the Society.

Christine Bell has been a member of the Society since 1976, and was President in 1995-6. Her interest in the locality led her to join the Local History Group at its inception in 1989, at which time she was following a study of Methodism and its associated chapels in the dales. Since then her growing interest in botany has developed, and she is now leader of the Botany Group.

Leslie Bloom lives in Pudsey and, as a member of the Society since the late 1950s, he has led many walks over a long period of time. He attended Arthur Raistrick's classes in Skipton for many years, became a close companion and joined many of Arthur's excursions. Until recently he has been Hon. Treasurer and Trustee of the Arthur Raistrick Memorial Lecture Fund. He has attended a number of courses on geology, archaeology, and history at the University of Leeds and the University of Bradford, living as he does between the two cities. As a Chartered Engineer he spent all his working life in the fuel and power industry – later as a Consultant, along with 14 years as a part-time lecturer in mathematics at Bradford Technical College (later part of the University) where he had originally qualified in Mechanical Engineering. In 2007 he was awarded Honorary Life Membership of the Society.

Jean Booth was born and brought up in Bradford. She gained an Honours degree in History from Nottingham University and then taught history before retiring to Grassington with her husband. Her particular interests have been population studies in Grassington associated with the Enclosure Award 1792, and the Tithe Award 1846. In 1999, whilst attending a series of lectures with The School of Continuing Education, The University of Leeds, she worked jointly with another Society member, June Tingey, to compile A Preliminary report on the Enclosure Act for Grassington dated 1792 and it's Effect on the Medieval Landscape (Society Archives).

Marjorie Budd, a member of the Society since 1970 and for many years arranged the summer walks programme.

Ruth Camm was a member of the Society between 1993 and 2000. After a working life in mathematics and lecturing she and her husband moved to Gargrave in 1987. They had lived in north-east Cheshire, close to the limestone countryside of Derbyshire - an area for walking, attractive villages and visible remains of smallscale lead mining, comparable and contemporary with the operations based in the Yorkshire Dales. It was through Arthur Raistrick that Ruth's interest in the Dales countryside and its history was kindled, along with a realisation that many local people were studying their surroundings and sharing their knowledge with others, not least through the Field Society.

Christine Chisholm daughter of Mollie and Robert Chisholm, founder members of the Vernacular Buildings Study group, joined the Society in 1974, and has been its Assistant Librarian for many years. Through her parents' bequest, and jointly with proceeds from the sale of books bequeathed by the family of Robert and Jacqueline Keighley, Christine enabled the Field Society to house their library books in a purpose built cupboard, specially designed by Peter Merrell, a Grassington cabinet-maker.

David Francis, Artist, was a Chartered Civil Engineer, a career which demanded a degree of draughtsmanship with an eye for detail, and this he developed as a means of recreation. His interest in architectural subjects and buildings in the landscape, together with the ways of rural life and methods of working, have extended his repertoire. Although he paints in oils, water colour is his favourite medium, together with pen and ink which enhances his love of detail. He exhibits with Buckden Art Group.

Carrie Gledhill was born in Bradford around 1890 and moved to Grassington in the 1920s. At one time she and her husband, who was known as Tommie Tinner, lived over the post office at the top of Main Street. While Tommy earned a modest living making useful household objects, such as oilstoves and suchlike, Carrie worked as a hairdresser. Her drawings form an interesting record of the village as it was at that time.

Richard Harland was born and brought up in Scarborough. He moved to Grassington in 1959 and became a member of the Field Society. In 1969 he was a Founding Secretary, with Arthur Raistrick as Chairman, of the Friends of Craven Museum. From 1959 he was Clerk and solicitor to the Craven Water Board, and from 1974 similarly to the Yorkshire Water Authority, until retirement in 1985. Through his membership and interest in the Society of Friends, he has researched and published several booklets on the history of Quakers and their Meeting Houses in Craven and Upper Wharfedale.

Jacqueline Keighley and her husband, Robert retired to Kilnsey in 1973 from medical practice in Leeds. While in retirement, he trained for the nonstipendiary Anglican ministry and Jacquie became a lay-reader. They were both very active on deanery and diocesan synods and in rural theological activities, while their home at Chapel House Lodge became a welcoming centre for study groups and discussions. They became dedicated to the Upper Wharfedale Field Society, each in turn taking office as President. Together, they inaugurated the Vernacular Building Study Group within the Society, and formed the initial association with the Yorkshire Vernacular Buildings Study Group. Jacquie was also a keen and knowledgeable bird-watcher. Their collection of books was given to the Field Society, some of these now forming part of the present library.

Martha Kneale, (nee Hurst) 1909-2001, was born in Skipton. She was a gifted pupil of the Girls' High School, a first class scholar at Somerville College, Oxford, and for 30 years a tutor of philosophy and a fellow at Lady Margaret Hall. She was married to William Kneale, also a philosophy don and later Oxford professor. In 1966 they returned to Wharfedale, living first in Burnsall and later moving to the terrace known as Bridge End in Grassington. Both Martha and William took an active part in local organisations, including the Workers Educational Association (WEA) where they shared their deep knowledge of English Literature with fellow students. Botany was Martha's great love. As a member of the Field Society Botany Group, her interpretations of Latin and Greek names were especially appreciated by lay members, and she was able to identify less common plants and grasses with authority. Trees were another of her delights. She had a personality of great gentleness, with a modest, easy style in her choice of words, and she was much valued for the scholarly content of her contributions to the Local History Group.

Helen Lefevre joined the Society in 1961, shortly after her retirement from Bradford Girls' High School where she had taught chemistry. Formerly, with a first class honours degree, she had been departmental head of science at Mansfield Girls' Grammar School. Helen held the post of Librarian for the UWFS for seven years before becoming Secretary for a further seven years, and at the same time, she led the Botany Group. She then became President, and was appointed an Honorary Life Member in recognition of 'her perseverance and untiring work for the Field Society'. (1979 Bulletin) For many years she was a member of the executive council of the Yorkshire Naturalists Union. Her botanical records were compiled over a period of fifty years, and were submitted for inclusion in county and national observations and surveys. As a member of the management committee of the Yorkshire Wildlife Trust, she became one of the first wardens of Grass Wood, and it was at this time that she chose Donald Whitehead's drawing of the flower Herb Paris, which grows locally in Grass Wood, to be adopted as the Society's logo. Having no garden around her cottage in Linton, she grew alpine plants in stone troughs by her front door, and she took great pleasure in painting and photographing wild flowers and local scenery.

Herbert Masterson was a regional chief officer of the Central Electricity Generating Board and a board member of the Yorkshire Water Authority. This article arose from the findings he published in the Yorkshire Archaeological Journal Volume 71, 1999 entitled 'An Electrical Undertaking in Upper Wharfedale'.

Phyllida Oates joined the Society in 1998 having retired from 28 years on the Black Isle, Scottish Highlands. She is a keen gardener, and became actively interested in various Field Society Groups, including Local History, Vernacular Architecture and Geology. She is a regular member of the Society's walking group, with whom she photographed some of the milestones and waymarkers still to be found along old coach and packhorse routes. In 2004 Phyllida became Speaker Secretary for the Field Society.

Dorothy Peake, 1935-1998 was a good friend of Jacqueline and Robert Keighley. They shared a strong Christian faith throughout the years Dorothy worked at Scargill House, near Kettlewell. Her composition 'Benedicite of the Dales' was sung at Jacquie's funeral service in Conistone Church.

Philip Sugden was born and brought up in Sutton in Craven, and first began work in Bradford where he studied at the University and trained as a Chartered Accountant. In his subsequent career in airport management he travelled to many parts of the world before moving to Grassington in 1993. Since that time he has been an active member of the UWFS, and has been its treasurer for many years until he became President 2005-6. Philip is a great walker, who also studied archaeology at

Craven College and his report is based upon a course-work project produced at that time.

Jean Reinsch was born in Threshfield, and has always lived in Upper Wharfedale, where she has a wide breadth of local knowledge and a great love of the Dales. David Johnson (UWFS), writing in Jean's published memoirs entitled 'The Dales are Mine' has described how 'For more years than she might care to remember' she arranged an annual programme of monthly walks throughout the Dales, leading many of them herself with her husband Kurt. *'Come rain, snow or gale these walks have enabled established residents and newcomers alike to explore the secrets of the landscape we are privileged to be part of '*. She was Treasurer of the UWFS for forty years, and is now an Honorary Life Member. A member of Arthur Raistrick's WEA classes in the 1960s, she was also a fell and rock climber, a potholer, and with Kurt, a founder member of the Upper Wharfedale Fell Rescue Association.

Bill Rhodes served an apprenticeship in electrical engineering in the West Riding in the late 1940s, when mills were being converted from steam to electrical power. For most of his working life he was employed by the BBC installing broadcasting equipment, but always retained a great affection for the giant steam engines he helped make redundant and which now exist only in industrial museums. This led to an interest in the time, almost a century earlier, when steam took over from the power of moving water. Newly retired in 1989, he joined the UWFS and the group led by Jacqueline Keighley to rediscover the sites of some of the watermills of Upper Wharfedale, making photography his contribution to the project.

(The project is not yet complete but the notes and photographs are retained and can be seen in the Society's Archives.)

Helen Wheatley was born in Tasmania in 1941. She studied Fine Arts at the Tasmanian School of Arts from 1959 to 1962. Having taught art at secondary level for three years in Tasmania, she changed course to work as a set designer in theatre and television. In 1969, she moved to London to join the BBC and worked on sets for the classic serials. Here Helen consolidated a long-term interest in architectural forms, as she learnt the techniques of architectural drawing. She has also been deputy Editor of 'Montessori International' and a Montessori teacher and teacher trainer. She has been responsible for editing this collection of articles.

Erratum

P. 77 Reference 2. Illustration (see figs. 29a and 29b)
not Fig. 27.

P. 85 Photograph caption for Fig. 32 should read Aerial view, Low Mill Lane
not Low Mill from Low Mill Lane.